Level D

# VOCABULARY CONNECTIONS

## A Content Area Approach

Program Consultants

**Dr. Barbara Coulter**
Director, Department of Communication Arts
Detroit Public Schools

**Dr. Catherine C. Hatala**
Director, Reading/English Language Arts
School District of Philadelphia

STECK-VAUGHN
C O M P A N Y
ELEMENTARY • SECONDARY • ADULT • LIBRARY

**Executive Editor:** Diane Sharpe
**Project Editor:** Amanda Johnson Sperry
**Assistant Art Director:** Richard Balsam
**Design Manager:** Jim Cauthron
**Photo Editor:** Margie Foster
**Product Development:** McClanahan & Company, Inc.
**Electronic Production:** Tracor Publications


## ILLUSTRATIONS

**Cover:** Ed Lindlof
**Content Area Logos:** Skip Sorvino

Donna Ayers 56–57, 84–87, 89, 104, 107; Heidi Chang 12–15, 17, 50, 52, 91–92, 94, 105, 108–109, 113; Nancy Didion 7–9, 11; Eldon Doty 31–33, 35; Leslie Dunlap 24–25, 28; Nancy Howard 18–20, 22; Pamela Johnson 36–39, 41, 71–72, 74, 76, 96–98, 100, 115–116, 118, 120–122, 124; Linda Knox 59; Bob Lange 48–49, 67–68, 70; Ann Neumann 43–44; 46; Marcia Sewall 60–63, 65, 80–81, 83.


## PHOTOGRAPHY

P. 5 Larry Lefever/Grant Heilman Photography; p. 6 Emil Schulthess/Black Star; p. 12 Bill Hampton; p. 23 Odile Noel/Sygma; p. 26 Laser Spectacles; p. 29 Larry Lefever/Grant Heilman Photography; p. 30 USDA Photo, Science Source/Photo Researchers; p. 42 George Porter, National Audubon Society/Photo Researchers; p. 47 Biophoto Associates/Photo Researchers; p. 53 Archive Photos; p. 54 Robert Azzi/Woodfin Camp & Associates; p. 55 Stock Boston; p. 66 NASA/Black Star; p. 73 Abbas/Magnum Photos; p. 77 Art Bilstein, National Audubon Society/Photo Researchers; pp.78–79 UPI/Bettmann/Corbis; p. 90 Keith Gunnar/Photo Researchers; p. 95 Allsport; p. 101 Topham/The Image Works; pp. 102–103, 105 Culver Pictures; p. 114 Movie Still Archives; p. 119 David Young-Wolff/PhotoEdit.


## ACKNOWLEDGMENTS

*Abingdon Press:* From *Thomas Alva Edison, Inventor*. Copyright renewal © 1981 by Ruth Cromer Weir Dimond. Used by permission of the publisher, Abingdon Press.

*HarperCollins Publishers*: Adaptation from Chapter 9 of *Stone Fox* by John Reynolds Gardiner. Text copyright © 1980 by John Reynolds Gardiner. Reprinted by permission of HarperCollins Publishers.

*Highlights for Children, Inc.*: "Mountain Mist" by Pam Sandlin from *Highlights for Children*, February 1988. Used by permission of Highlights for Children, Inc., Columbus, OH. Copyright © 1988.

*Macmillan Publishing Company*: Pronunciation Key, reprinted with permission of the publisher from the *Macmillan School Dictionary 2*. Copyright © 1990 Macmillan Publishing Company, a division of Macmillan, Inc.

*Pavilion Books Ltd.*: "The Mango Tree," from *Seasons of Splendour* by Madhur Jaffrey. Copyright © 1985 by Madhur Jaffrey. Reprinted by permission of Pavilion Books Ltd.

*Gail Provost*: from *Popcorn* by Gail and Gary Provost. Copyright © 1985 by Gail and Gary Provost. Reprinted by permission of Gail Provost.

ISBN 0-8172-6353-5

14 15 DBH 05 04 03

# TABLE OF CONTENTS

# TABLE OF CONTENTS

# BRIGHT LIGHTS

**The sun lights up the sky in the daytime. The moon and stars give us light at night. Electric light bulbs light up our homes. Our world is filled with light.**

In Lessons 1 - 4, you will read about different kinds of light. Think about where light comes from and how it is used. What words come to mind when you think about light? Write your words under the headings below.

| Where Light Comes From | How Light Is Used |
|---|---|
| _____ | _____ |
| _____ | _____ |
| _____ | _____ |
| _____ | _____ |
| _____ | _____ |

★ Read the story below. Think about the meanings of the **boldfaced** words. ★

# Land of the Midnight Sun

In most parts of the world, people depend on two **daily** events. They expect a **sunrise** every morning. And they expect a **sunset** every evening. But, people who live in the **Arctic** Circle do not depend on these daily events. At the icy northern tip of the world, dawn and **nightfall** do not come every day.

The Arctic Circle is near the North Pole. There, from March until September, the sun never drops below the **horizon**. Instead, it stays in the sky all night and all day. It shines with its usual **brightness**. That is why this area is known as "the land of the midnight sun."

This happens because of the **location** of the sun and the earth. The earth travels around the sun once each year. As the earth moves, sunlight hits different parts of it at different angles. The earth also spins. It makes one turn each day. This causes day and night in most parts of the world.

At the North Pole it is different. The earth's spinning does not always make the sun disappear from view. Instead, the sun stays overhead for six months. During that time, it is always daylight!

Not everyone would like to live around the North Pole. People would miss **twilight**. Twilight is the time of day when the sun has set before it gets completely dark. People also would miss seeing **moonlit** nights.

However, the people in "the land of the midnight sun" are not always without moonlight. They have moonlight during the other six months. Then it is dark all day and all night. During these months people spend most of their time indoors. They play games, study, and work to while away the hours of darkness.

★ Go back to the story. Underline the words or sentences that give you a clue to the meaning of each **boldfaced** word. ★

# USING CONTEXT

Meanings for the vocabulary words are given below. Go back to the story and read each sentence that has a vocabulary word. If you still cannot tell the meaning, look for clues in the sentences that come before and after the one with the vocabulary word. Write each word in front of its meaning.

| | | | |
|---|---|---|---|
| brightness | twilight | horizon | location |
| nightfall | sunset | daily | moonlit |
| sunrise | Arctic | | |

1. _____ : the region around the North Pole

2. _____ : the line where the earth and the sky meet

3. _____ : the time when the sun goes down; sundown

4. _____ : the time when the sun comes up in the morning; dawn

5. _____ : the time of day between sundown and complete darkness; dusk

6. _____ : happening every day

7. _____ : the coming of darkness at the end of the day

8. _____ : lighted by the moon

9. _____ : the place where someone or something is located

10. _____ : the quality of being bright

# COMPOUND WORDS

A **compound word** is made up of two or more words. For example, <u>sail</u> and <u>boat</u> make up the compound word <u>sailboat</u>. Join one word from Column A with one from Column B to make four compound words. Write the new words.

| Column A | Column B |
|----------|----------|
| moon | set |
| night | rise |
| sun | fall |
| sun | lit |

1. _____

2. _____

3. _____

4. _____

# CLOZE PARAGRAPH

Use the words in the box to complete the paragraphs. Reread the paragraphs to be sure they make sense.

| Arctic | location | brightness |
|--------|----------|------------|
| daily | twilight | horizon |

Eskimos are people who live in the cold lands of the

(1) _____. The (2) _____ of the Eskimos' land is very far north. So for part of the year, the sun's

(3) _____ lights the sky. Then

(4) _____ activities like fishing and hunting can be done all day and all night.

Later the sun sinks below the (5) _____.

The Eskimos watch the (6) _____ begin. They know darkness and winter will follow.

# WORD PUZZLE

Write a word from the box next to each clue. Then read the words formed by the letters in the squares. You will have the answer to this riddle.

Why did the mother enjoy waking her son?

She liked to see _____ _____ _____!

| daily | brightness | Arctic | nightfall |
| horizon | sunset | twilight | moonlit |
| sunrise | locations | | |

1. dim light before dark ☐ _ _ _ _ _ _

2. when darkness comes _ _ _ ☐ _ _ _ _

3. quality of being bright _ _ _ _ _ _ _ ☐ _

4. also called sundown ☐ _ _ _ _ _

5. lighted by the moon _ _ ☐ _ _ _ _

6. line where the earth and sky meet _ _ _ _ _ _ ☐

7. very cold region that is home to Eskimos and reindeer _ ☐ _ _ _ _

8. happening every day _ _ ☐ _ _

9. positions _ _ _ _ _ _ _ ☐ _

10. happening in the morning _ _ _ _ _ _ ☐

**Directions:** Fill in the space for the word that fits best in the sentence.

 Be sure to mark the answer space correctly. Do <u>not</u> mark the circle with an X or with a checkmark (✓). Instead, fill in the circle neatly and completely with your pencil.

1. I eat an apple every day. It is my _____ treat.
   ○ vegetable    ○ daily
   ○ Saturday    ○ arctic

2. It was between sundown and complete darkness. It was _____.
   ○ black    ○ sunrise
   ○ twilight    ○ morning

3. The day begins at dawn. Dawn is also called _____.
   ○ sunrise    ○ night
   ○ sunset    ○ afternoon

4. The sky is full of color as the sun goes down. It is _____.
   ○ sunrise    ○ morning
   ○ sunset    ○ noon

5. Reindeer live around the North Pole. They live in the _____.
   ○ jungle    ○ Arctic
   ○ twilight    ○ river

6. The night sky is bright. It is a _____ sky.
   ○ dark    ○ distant
   ○ sunrise    ○ moonlit

7. It is dark after sundown. _____ follows sundown.
   ○ Afternoon    ○ Nightfall
   ○ Morning    ○ Sunrise

8. The sky seems to meet the land. They meet at the _____.
   ○ horizon    ○ ocean
   ○ station    ○ twilight

9. The sun hurts my eyes today. Its _____ is blinding.
   ○ darkness    ○ distance
   ○ size    ○ brightness

10. We do not know where the store is. We forgot its _____.
   ○ owner    ○ brightness
   ○ location    ○ business

Imagine that you and your family took a summer trip to "the land of the midnight sun." Write a postcard to a friend. Tell about the sights you have seen. Use the postcard pictures on this page and the pictures in this lesson for ideas. Include some of the facts you have learned in the lesson.

On the lines below, write your postcard. Use some vocabulary words in your writing.

_____
(Date)

Dear _____ ,

_____

_____

_____

_____

_____

_____

_____

_____

_____

_____

_____

**Turn to "My Word List" on page 131. Write some words from the story or other words that you would like to know more about. Use a dictionary to find the meanings.**

_____

Your friend,

_____

★ Read the story below. Think about the meanings of the **boldfaced** words. ★

# The Magic Light

Thomas Alva Edison's life was filled with discovery and disappointment. His many inventions brought sound to our ears and light to our eyes. This is part of his story.

Thomas Edison was determined to make an electric light that would glow with heat. "I must make it **cheaply** enough for everybody to use," he said.

Edison had started one of the greatest inventions of all time. He hired a glass blower to make bulbs. He bought pumps to pump air out of the bulbs. And he thought of new ways to control electric current. He tried many materials to burn inside the bulbs. Sometimes he wondered if anything in the whole world could stand the **intense** heat necessary to **furnish** light.

For more than a year Edison worked on his light. Then one day he called in Charles Batchelor, one of his best scientists.

"Bring in the others who have worked on the light," he said.

The men crowded around as Edison turned on a switch and a bulb lighted. It gave off a bright white light.

"What's wrong with this?" asked one of the men.

"This light is not practical," answered Edison. "In the first place, it would cost too much. It took thirty feet of fine **platinum** wire rolled on a spool."

"Now watch while I turn the electricity a little stronger."

*Pfft!* Before their eyes, the light burned out. In less than a second the bulb had turned black. The stronger **current** had melted the platinum inside.

Edison went on to explain that in using platinum he had made an important discovery. "When the electricity is turned on, still more air can be pumped from the bulbs. While a bulb burns, we will pump it again. Then we will seal it tightly."

The men started to leave. Each felt new hope and confidence and pride. Each showed a new excitement.

"Wait, Batchelor," Edison said.

Just then an office boy rushed in. "Mrs. Edison said she couldn't imagine what you wanted with ordinary cotton sewing thread," he said. "But she gave it to me. Are you going to use thread in your new light?"

"Perhaps," smiled the **inventor**, reaching for the thread.

Quickly he cut off several small pieces. He bent each piece into a tiny loop shaped like a **horseshoe**.

"Carbonize these pieces of thread," Edison said to Batchelor. To carbonize them, the threads were baked in a hot oven until they were burned black.

"But I thought you had given up **carbon** for light." Batchelor was plainly surprised.

"I am going back to carbon," said Edison. "We can now pump more air from the bulbs. Carbon is still the best material I have found.

"Bring the thread to me as soon as it is done. I will be waiting. And have more bulbs made," Edison added.

Several hours later Batchelor brought the threads. Quickly Edison attached one in a glass bulb.

When the air was pumped out, the bulb was sealed. It was ready for the test. Edison turned on the electricity.

The bulb burned for forty hours. Even while it burned, the inventor was thinking of ways to improve it.

"Carbonized paper should work better than thread," he reasoned. He rolled paper into a thin little roll as fine as thread and sent it to be baked into carbon.

He was right. The paper carbon burned **indefinitely**! People began to read and hear the news of the wonderful light. "Edison is a **wizard**," they declared. "Now he has invented a magic light."

From Thomas Alva Edison:
Inventor, by Ruth Cromer Weir

★ Go back to the story. Underline any words or sentences that give you clues to the meanings of the **boldfaced** words. ★

# CONTEXT CLUES

Read each sentence. Look for clues to help you complete each sentence with a word from the box. Write the word on the line.

| | | | |
|---|---|---|---|
| wizard | indefinitely | carbon | inventor |
| current | horseshoe | cheaply | intense |
| furnish | platinum | | |

1. An _____ is someone who creates new things.

2. Thomas Edison was called a _____ because he was so clever and created so many new things.

3. Edison wanted to find a way to _____, or supply, people with an easy way to light their homes.

4. He wanted to make his light bulbs _____, so people would not have to pay a lot for them.

5. He was willing to work _____ to find a way to do this.

6. He did not want to use _____, a precious gray metal, because it would cost too much.

7. He needed a material that would let a strong flow, or _____, of electricity go through the light bulb.

8. He wanted a material that would give off a powerful, or _____, amount of light.

9. He found that _____, a black material left on objects that have been burned, worked best.

10. Do you think he had a U-shaped _____, a symbol of good luck, hanging in his workshop?

# ANALOGIES

An **analogy** shows how two words go together in the same way as two other words. A kitten is a baby cat and a puppy is a baby dog. So you could say: Kitten is to cat as puppy is to dog. Write the words from the box to complete the following analogies.

| | | |
|---|---|---|
| intense | horseshoe | platinum |
| cheap | inventor | |

1. Sneaker is to child as _____ is to horse.

2. Rose is to flower as _____ is to metal.

3. Singer is to sing as _____ is to invent.

4. Weak is to slight as strong is to _____.

5. Good is to bad as _____ is to expensive.

# DICTIONARY SKILLS

A dictionary can help you find out how to say a word. Turn to page 133 in the Dictionary. Use the **pronunciation key** to help you learn how to say the vocabulary words in ( ) in the sentences below. Write the regular spelling for each word in ( ).

1. You find (kär′bən) after a fire. _____

2. A river can also have a (kûr′ent). _____

3. I will (fûr′nish) apples to eat. _____

4. He may stay (in def′ə nit lē). _____

5. A (wiz′ərd) is a very clever person. _____

**Directions:** Read the phrase. Look for the word or words that have the same or almost the same meaning as the boldfaced word. Mark the answer space for your choice.

 Think about the meaning of the **boldfaced** word before you choose an answer. Don't be fooled by a word that looks like the **boldfaced** word.

1. **intense** heat
   - ○ moist
   - ○ strong
   - ○ weak
   - ○ instant

2. strong **current**
   - ○ flow
   - ○ curl
   - ○ athlete
   - ○ fossil

3. **furnish** the food
   - ○ eat
   - ○ cook
   - ○ supply
   - ○ freeze

4. ask the **inventor**
   - ○ creator
   - ○ pirate
   - ○ insect
   - ○ singer

5. delay **indefinitely**
   - ○ dangerously
   - ○ without ideas
   - ○ sadly
   - ○ without limits

6. **horseshoe** form
   - ○ L-shape
   - ○ Y-shape
   - ○ U-shape
   - ○ T-shape

7. **platinum** wire
   - ○ broken
   - ○ plain
   - ○ glass
   - ○ metal

8. use **carbon**
   - ○ rubber
   - ○ gold
   - ○ control
   - ○ burned material

9. a **wizard**
   - ○ costume
   - ○ clever person
   - ○ willow
   - ○ wild animal

10. bought **cheaply**
    - ○ today
    - ○ at low cost
    - ○ quickly
    - ○ at no cost

Review

1. at **sunset**
   - ○ noon
   - ○ sunrise
   - ○ sundown
   - ○ daylight

2. **daily** chores
   - ○ everyday
   - ○ morning
   - ○ terrible
   - ○ damp

3. his **location**
   - ○ attention
   - ○ position
   - ○ lodging
   - ○ business

4. beautiful **sunrise**
   - ○ twilight
   - ○ evening
   - ○ sunflower
   - ○ dawn

# Writing

Imagine that you are Thomas Edison. You have just invented the electric light bulb. Now you want people to buy your light bulbs.

On the lines below, write at least three reasons why your light bulbs are better to use than candles. Use some vocabulary words in your writing.

My light bulbs are better than candles because _____

_____

_____

_____

_____

_____

_____

_____

_____

_____

_____

_____

_____

_____

_____

_____

_____

**Turn to "My Word List" on page 131. Write some words from the story or other words that you would like to know more about. Use a dictionary to find the meanings.**

★ Read the story below. Think about the meanings of
the **boldfaced** words. ★

# Rainbows

A rainbow is an **arch** of colors in the sky. This curved shape is
formed when the sun shines after a **rainstorm**. You can see a
rainbow only at certain times. To **observe** it, you need to have
the sun behind you. The rain must be in front of you.

A rainbow is a **spectacular** sight. It makes people stare in
wonder. A rainbow has six colors — violet, blue, green, yellow,
orange, and red. These colors are also present in sunlight. But
they are very **vivid** in a rainbow. They appear brighter than
usual.

A rainbow forms because of what happens when light shines
on water. The sun shines on a **raindrop**. The water **reflects** the
light, or sends it back. The light is broken up into separate
colors.

Of course, the sun shines on many raindrops at once. Each
raindrop breaks the light into the same six colors. Together,
millions of raindrops form a **display** of colors called a rainbow.

Most people have seen rainbows in the sky. But they can
form in other places, too. A rainbow can form wherever light
shines on **moisture**, or wetness. Rainbows sometimes form in
small puddles on the ground. The puddles can be made of
water. But sometimes a rainbow is **visible** in a puddle of oil.
You can also see a rainbow in water that squirts out of a garden
hose.

Next time you see a rainbow, look at the colors. Can you
name them?

★ Go back to the story. Underline the words or sentences that give
you a clue to the meaning of each **boldfaced** word. ★

# USING CONTEXT

Meanings for the vocabulary words are given below. Go back to the story and read each sentence that has a vocabulary word. If you still cannot tell the meaning, look for clues in the sentences that come before and after the one with the vocabulary word. Write each word in front of its meaning.

| | | | |
|---|---|---|---|
| spectacular | observe | moisture | visible |
| rainstorm | reflects | display | vivid |
| raindrop | arch | | |

1. _____ : able to be seen

2. _____ : a storm with a lot of rain

3. _____ : show

4. _____ : a single drop of rain

5. _____ : very bright

6. _____ : striking; amazing

7. _____ : a curved shape

8. _____ : to watch

9. _____ : sends back, as in heat, light, or a picture

10. _____ : water in the air

## CHALLENGE YOURSELF

Name two things you <u>observe</u> on your way to school.

_____    _____

Name two things that are <u>vivid</u> in color.

_____    _____

# WORD GROUPS

Read each pair of words. Think about how they are alike. Write the word from the box that best completes each group.

| | | | |
|---|---|---|---|
| reflects | vivid | arch | moisture |
| observe | display | | |

**1.** curve, loop, _____

**2.** mirrors, returns, _____

**3.** watch, notice, _____

**4.** bright, brilliant, _____

**5.** water, steam, _____

**6.** show, exhibit, _____

# CLOZE PARAGRAPH

Use the words in the box to complete the paragraph. Reread the paragraph to be sure it makes sense.

| | | | |
|---|---|---|---|
| display | spectacular | moisture | visible |
| rainstorm | raindrop | | |

The air felt damp and full of (1) _____. We went on the picnic anyway. We got the food out. Then I felt one

(2) _____ fall on my head. Seconds later, a

(3) _____ was showering water on us. When it

was over, we saw a (4) _____ of colors in the

sky. A rainbow was (5) _____. The storm

ruined our picnic, but it treated us to a (6) _____ sight!

**Directions:** Read each sentence carefully. Then choose the best answer to complete each sentence. Mark the space for the answer you have chosen.

**Tip** Some tests have letters inside the answer circles. Fill in the circle next to your answer, covering the letter, too.

1. When a **rainstorm** is reported, you know there are _____.
   - (A) snows
   - (B) droughts
   - (C) showers
   - (D) suns

2. A **spectacular** movie is one that you will _____.
   - (A) ignore
   - (B) buy
   - (C) forget
   - (D) remember

3. A **vivid** painting has colors that are _____.
   - (A) boring
   - (B) bright
   - (C) bare
   - (D) big

4. When you **observe** something, you _____ it.
   - (A) touch
   - (B) break
   - (C) watch
   - (D) smell

5. **Moisture** in a cellar will make it _____.
   - (A) dry
   - (B) damp
   - (C) dark
   - (D) glow

6. An **arch** is a _____.
   - (A) curve
   - (B) color
   - (C) flag
   - (D) name

7. A **visible** object is one that can be _____.
   - (A) heard
   - (B) tasted
   - (C) seen
   - (D) walked

8. If a **raindrop** lands on you, you become _____.
   - (A) visible
   - (B) sleepy
   - (C) happy
   - (D) wet

9. When an object **reflects** light, the light _____.
   - (A) melts
   - (B) disappears
   - (C) goes home
   - (D) comes back

10. A **display** of art could be a _____ of paintings.
    - (A) collection
    - (B) bucket
    - (C) house
    - (D) city

*Writing*

A rainbow is not the only beautiful sight you can see in the sky. A sunrise can also be colorful, and so can a sunset. A full moon or a starry sky can also catch your attention.

Compare a rainbow to one of these other sky sights. Explain how they are alike and how they are different. Think about things such as how they look and what time of day you see them. Also think about how often you see them and how long they stay in the sky. Use the pictures and facts from the story to help you. Use some vocabulary words in your writing.

_____

_____

_____

_____

_____

_____

_____

_____

_____

_____

_____

_____

**Turn to "My Word List" on page 131. Write some words from the story or other words that you would like to know more about. Use a dictionary to find the meanings.**

★ Read the story below. Think about the meanings of the **boldfaced** words. ★

# Lights! Lasers! Action!

Brightly colored beams of light fly through the air. Some of them form shapes such as circles and triangles. Others form more lifelike images. They make **realistic** pictures of people and animals. Welcome to a laser light show!

Lasers are tools that **produce** very powerful beams of light. The light that a laser makes is so strong that it can cut a diamond. What makes laser light so powerful? It is very narrow, so it doesn't spread out as it travels. Doctors use lasers. For example, a **physician** can use the beam to cut like a knife. Businesses use them to power machines. In light shows, lasers also have an **artistic** use. They are used to create beauty.

The first laser light show took place in 1973 in the United States. Since then, people have been held **spellbound** by the colors and patterns in these displays. They find it difficult to take their eyes away from the magical beams. In today's laser light shows, the people who control the lasers often **focus** the beams on a wall. Aiming the beam at the wall **transforms** it into a movie screen for laser light pictures. Sometimes the laser **operators** direct the light at mirrors placed around the area. Each mirror reflects the beam onto another mirror for a dazzling effect.

Laser light shows can be found at many theme parks, plays, and sporting events. People around the world **marvel** at the exciting displays. They are filled with wonder as a dark sky suddenly comes alive with dancing lights. Laser light shows **impress** everyone who watches them. They leave people amazed by their magic.

★ Go back to the story. Underline the words or sentences that give you a clue to the meaning of each **boldfaced** word. ★

# CONTEXT CLUES

Read each sentence. Look for clues to help you complete each sentence with a word from the box. Write the word on the line.

| | | | |
|---|---|---|---|
| physician | focus | operators | artistic |
| spellbound | transforms | realistic | produce |
| marvel | impress | | |

1. Lasers are machines that _____ very strong beams of light.

2. A _____ can use a laser beam to cut like a knife.

3. The people who create laser light shows use their

   _____ talents to create beautiful pictures.

4. In a laser light show, laser beams can be used to create

   very _____ pictures of people.

5. The people who create shows with laser lights can

   _____ the beams on walls and mirrors.

6. Laser light directed at a wall _____, or changes, the wall into a movie screen.

7. Many people _____ at the light and color created by laser beams.

8. Some people are so _____ by laser light shows that they stare at the designs for a long time.

9. The job of laser _____ is to control the beams.

10. The magical light and color of a laser light show are sure

    to _____ anyone!

# REWRITING SENTENCES

Rewrite each sentence using one of the vocabulary words.

| produce | physician | transforms |
|---------|-----------|------------|

1. You should see a doctor about that cut on your knee.

   _____

2. In this fairy tale, the kiss from a princess changes a frog into a prince.

   _____

3. Our town has a factory that uses iron to make steel.

   _____

# MULTIPLE MEANINGS

The words in the box have more than one meaning. Look for clues in each sentence to tell which meaning is being used. Write the letter of the meaning next to the correct sentence.

| impress | produce | focus |
|---------|---------|-------|
| **a.** make a mark on | **a.** fresh fruit and vegetables | **a.** concentrate |
| **b.** amaze | **b.** to bring forth | **b.** aim light beams |

_____ 1. We can impress the wax because it is soft.

_____ 2. A great movie will impress many people.

_____ 3. A hamster can produce babies every eight weeks.

_____ 4. We bought produce and meat at the grocery store.

_____ 5. Tonight I need to focus on my homework.

_____ 6. You can use a magnifying glass to focus sunlight.

# ANALOGIES

Remember that an **analogy** shows how two words go together in the same way as two other words. Write the words from the box to complete the following analogies.

| impress | marvel | artistic | produce |
|---------|--------|----------|---------|

1. Know is to understand as _____ is to wonder.

2. Whisper is to yell as _____ is to destroy.

3. Musical is to music as _____ is to artist.

4. Scare is to frighten as _____ is to amaze.

# DICTIONARY SKILLS

Write the words in alphabetical order, one word one each line. Then turn to the Dictionary, beginning on page 133. Find each word in the Dictionary. Write its meaning below.

| physician operators | spellbound realistic | focus artistic | transforms impress |
|---------|--------|----------|---------|

1. _____

2. _____

3. _____

4. _____

5. _____

6. _____

7. _____

8. _____

**Directions:** Fill in the space for the word that fits best in the sentence.

 **Tip** Read the first sentence carefully. It will help you choose the missing word in the second sentence.

1. My uncle wants to practice medicine. He plans to be a _____.
   A ○ physician     C ○ coach
   B ○ lawyer        D ○ child

2. Sara drew a lifelike picture of her mother. It looked very _____.
   A ○ green         C ○ messy
   B ○ realistic     D ○ tired

3. That is an auto factory. It can _____ many cars each day.
   A ○ laugh         C ○ produce
   B ○ drive         D ○ grow

4. Those people control the machines. They are the _____.
   A ○ persons       C ○ doctors
   B ○ actors        D ○ operators

5. I can't find my way in the dark. Please _____ the flashlight over here.
   A ○ focus         C ○ remove
   B ○ break         D ○ finish

6. The campers are surprised to see so many stars. They _____ at the sight.
   A ○ stop          C ○ marvel
   B ○ match         D ○ sleep

7. The boy drew and painted all the posters for the show. He has a lot of _____ talent.
   A ○ weak          C ○ mechanical
   B ○ artistic      D ○ awful

8. That movie is the best one I have ever seen. It will really _____ you.
   A ○ sadden        C ○ impress
   B ○ annoy         D ○ bore

9. The new coat of paint makes a big change. It _____ this room.
   A ○ chooses       C ○ builds
   B ○ cleans        D ○ transforms

10. I could hardly move when I heard the music. I was _____ by the melody.
    A ○ wakened      C ○ spellbound
    B ○ framed       D ○ lost

**Review**

1. The painting is very bright. It has _____ colors.
   A ○ purple        C ○ vivid
   B ○ angry         D ○ dull

2. We watched in amazement. It was a _____ sunset.
   A ○ late          C ○ normal
   B ○ silent        D ○ spectacular

Suppose that you can create your own laser light show. You can decide where to have it. You can also choose the colors and shapes to use and the pictures to show. You can tell a story. You can make the lights change quickly or slowly.

On the lines below, tell about your laser light show. Use some vocabulary words in your writing.

_____

_____

_____

_____

_____

_____

_____

_____

_____

_____

_____

_____

_____

_____

_____

**Turn to "My Word List" on page 131. Write some words from the story or other words that you would like to know more about. Use a dictionary to find the meanings.**

★ To review the words in Lessons 1–4, turn to page 125. ★

# CYCLES OF CHANGE

It is autumn, and this maple tree will soon lose its leaves. It will be bare in the winter. What will happen next in the maple tree's cycle of change?

In Lessons 5 - 8, you will read about growth and change. Think about what grows and changes. A silkworm changes into a moth. A seed becomes a plant. We change, too. Write your ideas on the lines below.

| Begins As | Changes To |
|-----------|------------|
| _____ | _____ |
| _____ | _____ |
| _____ | _____ |
| _____ | _____ |
| _____ | _____ |

★ Read the story below. Think about the meanings of the **boldfaced** words. ★

# An Island Is Born

Before 1963, there was no Surtsey Island. Then one day, Surtsey came right out of the ocean! Many islands are formed in this way as volcanoes grow on the ocean floor.

What is a volcano? And how does one form an island? It starts deep inside the earth. There, the heat is so great that, like a giant **furnace**, it melts rock. This **molten** rock joins with gases and rises up under the ground. If the push upward is great enough, it can make an opening in the earth's surface. Because so much of the earth is covered by oceans, many of these openings appear under the water.

When a volcano **erupts**, the melted rock is thrown up into the water. This **lava** drops back to the ocean floor. There it cools into rock again. And slowly it builds a mountain. As more melted rock is thrown out, it flows down the sides of the mountain. Hard rock is formed on these **slopes**, building up land that grows higher as it spreads wider. Finally, after what may take many years, the mountain reaches the water's surface. It seems to appear suddenly as a tiny island. Still the hot rock **overflows** onto the top of the mountain, adding more land above the water.

In time, the island grows large enough for many people to settle on it. Some of the Hawaiian Islands were formed this way. The volcano may remain **active**, spitting fire and melted rock. In that case, the people must learn to live with this danger. They learn the signs, or **warnings**, that tell when the volcano will erupt. When they feel rumblings in the earth, the people **flee**. They run to find **refuge** on a safer part of the island. There they must wait until the volcano is quiet again.

★ Go back to the story. Underline the words or sentences that give you a clue to the meaning of each **boldfaced** word. ★

# USING CONTEXT

Meanings for the vocabulary words are given below. Go back to the story and read each sentence that has a vocabulary word. If you still cannot tell the meaning, look for clues in the sentences that come before and after the one with the vocabulary word. Write each word in front of its meaning.

| | | | |
|---|---|---|---|
| molten | refuge | active | overflows |
| furnace | lava | slopes | warnings |
| erupts | flee | | |

1. _____ : melted rock from a volcano

2. _____ : signals or signs that tell of danger

3. _____ : a closed-in space in which heat is produced

4. _____ : melted by heat

5. _____ : to run away from danger

6. _____ : working; showing action

7. _____ : sides of hills or mountains

8. _____ : a place that provides protection

9. _____ : runs over the top or brim

10. _____ : bursts out; releases suddenly

## CHALLENGE YOURSELF

Name two <u>warnings</u> you might hear on a weather report.

_____     _____

Volcanoes are <u>active</u>, but so are you. Name two active things you do.

_____     _____

# SYNONYMS

Remember that **synonyms** are words that have the same or almost the same meaning. Match the words in the box with their synonyms listed below. Write each word on the line.

| overflows | refuge | erupts | warning |
|-----------|--------|--------|---------|

1. caution _____

2. floods _____

3. explodes _____

4. shelter _____

# DICTIONARY SKILLS

**Guide words** are the two words at the top of each dictionary page. They show the first and last entries on that page. All the word entries in between are in alphabetical order. Look at the pairs of guide words. On the lines below each pair, write the words from the box that would appear on the same dictionary page. Be sure to put them in alphabetical order.

| slopes | active | lava | furnace |
|--------|--------|------|---------|
| flee   | molten |      |         |

**ability / game**

1. _____

2. _____

3. _____

**lady / sudden**

4. _____

5. _____

6. _____

# CROSSWORD PUZZLE

Use the clues and the words in the box to complete the crossword puzzle.

| erupts | warnings | flee | furnace | active |
| refuge | molten | lava | slopes | overflows |

## Across

**2.** to run away
**6.** melted rock
**7.** on the go
**8.** hillsides
**9.** safe place

## Down

**1.** spills over
**2.** a very hot place
**3.** blows up
**4.** melted by heat
**5.** danger signals

# GET WISE TO TESTS

**Directions:** Fill in the space for the word or words that have the same or almost the same meaning as the boldfaced word.

 Think about the meaning of the **boldfaced** word before you choose an answer. Don't be fooled by a word that looks like the **boldfaced** word.

1. **active** player
   - ○ actual
   - ○ working
   - ○ sleeping
   - ○ huge

2. sudden **warnings**
   - ○ tears
   - ○ warriors
   - ○ songs
   - ○ signals

3. seeks **refuge**
   - ○ repair
   - ○ shelter
   - ○ gifts
   - ○ people

4. **molten** rock
   - ○ magic
   - ○ cooled
   - ○ black
   - ○ melted

5. metal **furnace**
   - ○ heating space
   - ○ cooling space
   - ○ watering place
   - ○ furniture

6. hot **lava**
   - ○ dirt
   - ○ lace
   - ○ melted rock
   - ○ small rocks

7. volcano **erupts**
   - ○ explodes
   - ○ hardens
   - ○ quiets
   - ○ escapes

8. **flee** danger
   - ○ go toward
   - ○ run from
   - ○ weed out
   - ○ fight

9. mountain **slopes**
   - ○ spirits
   - ○ insects
   - ○ goats
   - ○ sides

10. lake **overflows**
    - ○ floods
    - ○ colors
    - ○ heats
    - ○ outruns

## Review

1. **focus** the light
   - ○ see
   - ○ color
   - ○ aim
   - ○ darken

2. **transforms** the room
   - ○ tramples
   - ○ changes
   - ○ likes
   - ○ lives in

3. see a **physician**
   - ○ doctor
   - ○ lawyer
   - ○ plumber
   - ○ banker

4. **spellbound** audience
   - ○ splendid
   - ○ fascinated
   - ○ angry
   - ○ bored

# *Writing*

Imagine that you are on vacation in Hawaii. You go to visit Mauna Loa, the biggest volcano. Just as you are about to take a picture, the mountain rumbles. You escape to safety, but you are close enough to see the volcano erupt.

Write an article for the school newspaper telling about your adventure. Describe what you saw and heard when the volcano erupted. Use the picture to help you include details. Use some vocabulary words in your writing.

_____

_____

_____

_____

_____

_____

_____

_____

_____

_____

_____

_____

_____

_____

**Turn to "My Word List" on page 131. Write some words from the story or other words that you would like to know more about. Use a dictionary to find the meanings.**

★ Read the story below. Think about the meanings of the **boldfaced** words. ★

# The Mango Tree

In this legend from India, a girl shows a special kind of love for her brother and her mango tree.

In a small town, there was a small house in which lived a young man, his wife, and the young man's sister. This small house had a small garden at the back in which grew a small **mango** tree. One day the young man's wife came to him and said, "Look here, I'm fed up with our situation."

"Have you come to complain about my sister again? Don't go on," said the brother. "I've heard it all before."

"And what does your lazy sister do all day? Nothing. She lolls about in the garden, watering her mango tree, talking to it, clearing away dead leaves, and feeding it **mulch**."

"That isn't all she does. She comes in and talks to me."

"Just because she **adores** you, doesn't mean you should **ignore** her faults. You must tell her to leave that silly mango tree alone, and come and help me with the housework. I really think we should marry her off."

A marriage was arranged. When all the ceremonies were over, and the sister was about to leave with her groom to lead a new life in a new town, she turned to her sister-in-law and said, "Dearest sister-in-law, I'm going to miss my mango tree so much. Would you please do me a great favor and look after it for me?"

"Oh, well, yes, yes," answered the sister-in-law.

Once the sister had left, the sister-in-law turned to her husband and yelled, "Did you hear that? She didn't say that she was going to miss you. She didn't say that she was going to miss me." The sister-in-law decided then that she was going to ignore the mango tree. Now she could be rid of both.

As the days passed, the unwatered, uncared for mango tree started drying up and its leaves began to fall.

At the same time, the brother, who had been a strong, **robust** and healthy young man, began to lose his **appetite** and get thinner and weaker.

One day a letter arrived. It was from the sister and said, "I hope all is well and that my tree is green and that my brother is in good health."

The remaining leaves of the mango tree were quite yellow by this time, but the sister-in-law wrote back, "Dearest sister. Your tree is fine, but your brother has not been feeling so good."

Soon another letter arrived from the sister. "Are you sure my tree is green? And how is my brother?"

The mango tree had only one brown leaf left on it now, and the brother was so sick that the doctors had said that he could not live. So the sister-in-law wrote back, "Your tree is fine, but the doctors have given up all hopes for your brother."

When the sister received this letter, she raced back to her small **hometown** and went straight into the small garden to water her tree. As she watered, cleared the weeds around it, and mulched it, it began slowly to turn green.

The brother, too, began to **recover**.

As more leaves returned to the tree, the brother's cheeks got pinker and his eyes became brighter. Within a month, the tree was healthy and strong.

And so was the brother.

It was only then that the sister turned to her sister-in-law and said, "Now do you understand? It was not the tree that I loved, but my brother. It was not the tree whose **welfare** I was concerned with, but my brother's. The tree and my brother share a common **soul**. It was my duty to look after them both.

From *Seasons of Splendour:*
*Tales, Myths & Legends of*
*India,* by Madhur Jaffrey

★ Go back to the story. Underline any words or sentences that give you clues to the meanings of the **boldfaced** words. ★

# CONTEXT CLUES

Read each sentence. Look for clues to help you complete each sentence with a word from the box. Write the word on the line.

| | | | |
|---|---|---|---|
| hometown | recover | welfare | appetite |
| robust | ignore | soul | adores |
| mango | mulch | | |

1. A _____ is a kind of fruit.

2. A mango tree needs _____, a covering of straw, leaves, and the like, to grow well.

3. The sister believes the tree and her brother share the same spirit or _____.

4. She _____ her brother, but she shows her love by caring for the tree.

5. She cares about her brother's _____ and wants him to be healthy and happy.

6. She would never _____ the tree, because not paying attention to it would hurt her brother.

7. Her brother loses his _____ and doesn't want to eat when the tree is not fed.

8. Her healthy, _____ brother becomes very ill.

9. She rushes back to her _____, the place where she lived as a child.

10. She helps her brother _____, or get back, his health by caring for the mango tree.

# MULTIPLE MEANINGS

The words in the box have more than one meaning. Look for clues in each sentence to tell which meaning is being used. Write the letter of the meaning next to the correct sentence.

| soul | appetite | recover |
|------|----------|---------|
| **a.** a person's spirit | **a.** longing for food | **a.** get back |
| **b.** a person | **b.** wish for something | **b.** make up for |

_____ **1.** There was not a <u>soul</u> around the old house.

_____ **2.** Those words come from his <u>soul</u>.

_____ **3.** He has such an <u>appetite</u>, he could eat a horse!

_____ **4.** She has an <u>appetite</u> for travel, but not the money.

_____ **5.** Can you <u>recover</u> the lost time by studying more?

_____ **6.** Did the police <u>recover</u> the money stolen from her?

# CLASSIFYING

Write each word from the box in the group where it belongs.

| welfare | hometown | ignore | mulch |
|---------|----------|--------|-------|
| robust | adore | mango | |

Plant words _____  _____

Health words _____  _____

Action word _____

Place word _____

Feeling word _____

# GET WISE TO TESTS

**Directions:** Read each sentence carefully. Then choose the best answer to complete each sentence. Mark the space for the answer you have chosen.

 If you are not sure which word completes the sentence, do the best you can. Try to choose the answer that makes the most sense.

1. To **recover** is to _____ your good health.
   (A) lose
   (B) get back
   (C) forget
   (D) get out

2. **An appetite** is a longing for _____.
   (A) food
   (B) sleep
   (C) light
   (D) quiet

3. **Mulch** is used in a _____.
   (A) garden
   (B) bedroom
   (C) lake
   (D) window

4. When someone **adores** you, the person _____ you.
   (A) hates
   (B) bakes
   (C) angers
   (D) loves

5. If you **ignore** someone, you do not pay _____ to him.
   (A) dimes
   (B) cake
   (C) attention
   (D) socks

6. A **mango** is a kind of _____.
   (A) dog
   (B) dance
   (C) fruit
   (D) meat

7. Your **hometown** is the place where you _____.
   (A) run
   (B) drive by
   (C) grow up
   (D) vacation

8. A **robust** person is _____.
   (A) wealthy
   (B) healthy
   (C) sickly
   (D) deadly

9. The **soul** is the spirit of _____.
   (A) money
   (B) time
   (C) color
   (D) life

10. A person who worries about your **welfare** cares about your _____.
    (A) dog
    (B) health and happiness
    (C) flowers
    (D) songs and dance

# Writing

In "The Mango Tree," the sister is concerned about her brother's welfare. She shows her concern by caring for the mango tree.

   On the lines below, describe a time when you were concerned about someone's welfare. Tell what you did to show your concern. Use some vocabulary words in your writing.

_____

_____

_____

_____

_____

_____

Turn to "My Word List" on page 131. Write some words from the story or other words that you would like to know more about. Use a dictionary to find the meanings.

_____

_____

★ Read the story below. Think about the meanings of
the **boldfaced** words. ★

# From Tadpole to Frog

Did you know that there are more than 2,000 types of frogs?
Some live on or near water all the time. Others **inhabit** land.
They live there most of their lives.

People who study animals are called **biologists**. They have
found that one thing is the same about all frogs. Each begins as
a tadpole. The tadpole is one stage in a frog's **development**. It
follows the egg stage.

A tadpole is not fully formed when it hatches. This is an
early stage of its **growth**. It lives in the water. Most tadpoles
can be found in **lagoons**. Some live in other quiet bodies of
water.

The tadpole breathes through **gills**. It is like a fish. In some
ways it is more like a fish than like a land animal. That is why
water is the best **environment** for it to live in at this stage of its
life.

The tadpole's body goes through slow, **gradual** changes as
it grows. First, the tail gets longer. Then the tadpole can swim.
It **darts** around in the water, moving quickly to find food. It
eats underwater plants called **algae**.

Soon, the tadpole's body grows legs. At this point, it also
loses its gills. It does all its breathing on land. The tadpole can
do this because its gills have been replaced by lungs.

The last change for the tadpole has to do with its tail. When
it first hatches, the tail is the longest part of its body. Over time,
the tail gets shorter and shorter. Soon, the tail is gone, and the
animal becomes a frog.

★ Go back to the story. Underline the words or sentences that give
you a clue to the meaning of each **boldfaced** word. ★

# CONTEXT CLUES

Read each sentence. Choose a word from the box that means the same as the underlined part of each sentence. Write the word on the line after the sentence.

| | | | |
|---|---|---|---|
| gills | development | growth | lagoons |
| inhabit | environment | algae | darts |
| gradual | biologists | | |

1. <u>Scientists who study animals</u> sort the frog family into two groups, frogs and toads. _____

2. Most frogs are found in <u>shallow bodies of water.</u> _____

3. Toads <u>live in</u> dry places on land. _____

4. A frog's <u>natural changes caused by growing</u> are interesting. _____

5. In one stage of <u>the process of growing</u>, a frog is called a tadpole. _____

6. It has <u>breathing organs</u> in its head. _____

7. It feeds on <u>underwater plants.</u> _____

8. <u>Slow but steady changes</u> happen as the tadpole grows larger. _____

9. Now it <u>moves quickly</u> everywhere. _____

10. In this friendly <u>setting</u>, a tadpole will grow into a frog. _____

# CHALLENGE YOURSELF

Name two animals that <u>inhabit</u> <u>lagoons</u>.

# SCIENCE WORDS

The words in the box all have to do with the science that studies plant and animal life. Write each word beside its meaning.

| | | |
|---|---|---|
| development | algae | environment |
| biologist | inhabit | |

**1.** to live in a place or area _____

**2.** small plants found underwater _____

**3.** natural stages in growing _____

**4.** surroundings that affect living things _____

**5.** person who studies animal and plant life _____

# ANALOGIES

Remember that an **analogy** shows how two words go together in the same way as two other words. Write the words from the box to complete the following analogies.

| growth | lagoons | gills | gradual | darts |
|---|---|---|---|---|

**1.** Lungs are to people as _____ are to fish.

**2.** Hills are to dirt as _____ are to water.

**3.** Runs is to horse as _____ is to tadpole.

**4.** Slow is to fast as _____ is to sudden.

**5.** Build is to house as _____ is to person.

# GET WISE TO TESTS

**Directions:** Read each sentence. Pick the word that best completes the sentence. Mark the letter for that word.

 Read carefully. Use the other words in the sentence to help you choose the missing word.

1. Some frogs _____ small ponds.
   A ○ dig          C ○ tadpole
   B ○ inhabit      D ○ bury

2. _____ study frogs.
   A ○ Jump         C ○ Biologists
   B ○ Science      D ○ Plants

3. The process is slow and _____.
   A ○ hatch        C ○ quickly
   B ○ gone         D ○ gradual

4. Fish breathe through _____.
   A ○ gills        C ○ nothing
   B ○ watering     D ○ biologists

5. A pond is a good _____ for a frog.
   A ○ inhabit      C ○ homely
   B ○ station      D ○ environment

6. Frogs like ponds and _____.
   A ○ dances       C ○ darts
   B ○ lagoons      D ○ cities

7. _____ is the process of getting larger.
   A ○ Growth       C ○ Remembering
   B ○ Death        D ○ Go

8. Tadpoles eat _____.
   A ○ shell        C ○ nothing
   B ○ quickly      D ○ algae

9. A frog's _____ is how it changes.
   A ○ friend       C ○ development
   B ○ follows      D ○ environments

10. When a fish _____, it moves quickly.
    A ○ creeps      C ○ swimming
    B ○ pond        D ○ darts

## Review

1. He is strong and _____.
   A ○ weak         C ○ happily
   B ○ robust       D ○ soul

2. We visited my mother's _____.
   A ○ appetite     C ○ hometown
   B ○ friendly     D ○ oceans

3. She will _____ her health.
   A ○ locate       C ○ lost
   B ○ ignoring     D ○ recover

4. A _____ is a kind of fruit.
   A ○ mango        C ○ cry
   B ○ carrot       D ○ mulch

## Writing

Did you know that a butterfly is like a frog in some ways? A butterfly also begins life looking completely different from the way it looks when it is full-grown. A butterfly begins as a tiny egg. The egg hatches into a caterpillar. The caterpillar eats lots of leaves. When it is time, the caterpillar spins a kind of shell around itself. After many days, a butterfly comes out of this shell.

Use the story and the pictures on this page to compare a butterfly to a frog. Think about how they are alike and different. Use some vocabulary words in your writing.

A frog and a butterfly both begin their lives as tiny

eggs. _____

_____

_____

_____

_____

_____

_____

_____

_____

_____

_____

_____

_____

_____

_____

**Turn to "My Word List" on page 131. Write some words from the story or other words that you would like to know more about. Use a dictionary to find the meanings.**

★ Read the story below. Think about the meanings of the **boldfaced** words. ★

# How Does Your Skin Grow?

As you grow, your skin grows, too. In fact, throughout your **lifetime** your skin keeps growing. Stare at your arm for about 60 seconds. Can you see any change? Probably not. Now, with your fingernail, gently **scrape** the surface of your skin. What you see are tiny specks that are flakes of skin cells. This is quite **normal**. Every hour your body sheds about one million dead skin cells.

Skin is strong and tough. It protects the muscles and organs underneath. It also keeps dangerous germs from entering the body. What keeps your skin strong? Do you know how your skin grows?

Skin is made up of three layers. Each layer has a **function**, or a different job to do. The bottom layer is thick and holds sweat **glands** and **nerves**, which help you feel. The sweat glands **insulate**, or keep the body from getting too hot. Cells in the glands make sweat. Sweat reaches the surface of the skin and dries, keeping you cool.

The middle layer of your skin has millions of cells. These cells grow and divide into other cells. As new cells are made, some are pushed to the top layer. The cells pushed to the surface are dead skin cells. The dead layer of skin rubs off. Then a new layer of skin takes its place. This keeps your skin **healthy**. Your skin keeps growing this way even as a **mature** adult.

Imagine, every month you have an almost completely new outer skin! It would be truly amazing to watch this change happen. But the growth and change of skin is **invisible** to the naked eye.

★ Go back to the story. Underline the words or sentences that give you a clue to the meaning of each **boldfaced** word. ★

# USING CONTEXT

Meanings for the vocabulary words are given below. Go back to the story and read each sentence that has a vocabulary word. If you still cannot tell the meaning, look for clues in the sentences that come before and after the one with the vocabulary word. Write each word in front of its meaning.

| lifetime | healthy | invisible | insulate |
|----------|---------|-----------|----------|
| glands | mature | function | scrape |
| nerves | normal | | |

1. _____ : the length of a person's life

2. _____ : to scratch from the surface

3. _____ : usual condition

4. _____ : groups of cells that alert the body to feel heat, cold, and pain

5. _____ : purpose

6. _____ : organs that produce materials used by the body

7. _____ : to protect something from getting too hot or too cold

8. _____ : well; fit

9. _____ : not able to be seen

10. _____ : full-grown; developed

## CHALLENGE YOURSELF

Name two things you can do to keep your skin <u>healthy</u>.

_____    _____

Name two things that <u>insulate</u> your body from the cold.

_____    _____

# SYNONYMS

**Synonyms** are words that have the same or almost the same meaning. Match the words in the box with their synonyms listed below. Write each word on the line.

| invisible | scrape | healthy |
|-----------|--------|---------|
| function | normal | mature |

**1.** usual _____

**2.** job _____

**3.** unseen _____

**4.** fit _____

**5.** full-grown _____

**6.** scratch _____

# WRITING SENTENCES

Use each vocabulary word in the box to write an original sentence.

| insulate | mature | nerves |
|----------|--------|--------|
| lifetime | glands | healthy |

**1.** _____

**2.** _____

**3.** _____

**4.** _____

**5.** _____

**6.** _____

# WORD MAP

Use the vocabulary words in the box to complete the word map about the human body. Add other words that you know to each group. One heading will not have any vocabulary words, but only your words.

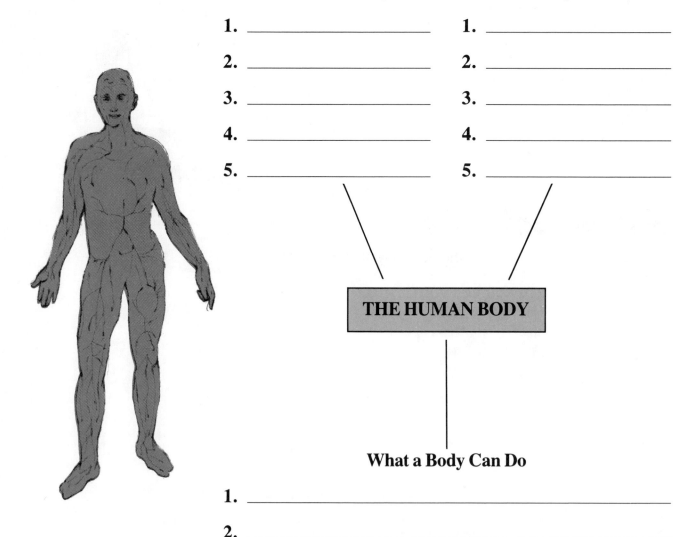

| mature | normal | glands | healthy | nerves |

**Parts of the Body**

1. _____
2. _____
3. _____
4. _____
5. _____

**How a Body Can Look**

1. _____
2. _____
3. _____
4. _____
5. _____

**THE HUMAN BODY**

**What a Body Can Do**

1. _____
2. _____
3. _____
4. _____
5. _____

**Directions:** Read the phrase. Look for the word or words that have the same or almost the same meaning as the boldfaced word. Mark the answer space for your choice.

 **Tip** Think about the meaning of the **boldfaced** word before you choose an answer. Don't be fooled by a word that looks like the **boldfaced** word.

1. sweat **glands**
   - ○ hairs
   - ○ strands
   - ○ organs
   - ○ waters

2. **mature** adult
   - ○ awake
   - ○ happy
   - ○ young
   - ○ full-grown

3. important **function**
   - ○ forecast
   - ○ purpose
   - ○ day
   - ○ success

4. **invisible** star
   - ○ unseen
   - ○ fading
   - ○ interesting
   - ○ valuable

5. **insulate** a house
   - ○ search
   - ○ look for
   - ○ protect
   - ○ inspire

6. **healthy** cat
   - ○ helpless
   - ○ sleepy
   - ○ wealthy
   - ○ well

7. long **lifetime**
   - ○ dream
   - ○ length of life
   - ○ lightning
   - ○ end of life

8. **normal** day
   - ○ usual
   - ○ long
   - ○ northern
   - ○ important

9. **scrape** a knee
   - ○ rest
   - ○ bend
   - ○ scold
   - ○ scratch

10. **nerves** feel
    - ○ nephews
    - ○ body parts
    - ○ plants
    - ○ car parts

## Review

1. **inhabit** lakes
   - ○ buy
   - ○ harm
   - ○ involve
   - ○ live in

2. **gradual** change
   - ○ slow
   - ○ great
   - ○ quiet
   - ○ quick

3. animal **darts**
   - ○ walks
   - ○ moves quickly
   - ○ dozes
   - ○ laughs a lot

4. fish **gills**
   - ○ eyes
   - ○ grim looks
   - ○ fins
   - ○ breathing organs

*Writing*

Your skin stays healthy by getting rid of dead cells. There are things that you can do, too, to help keep your skin in good health.

Look at the pictures. Use those ideas and others you have to write rules for taking care of your skin. Use some vocabulary words in your writing.

Rule 1: You should keep your skin healthy by _____

_____

_____

_____

_____

_____

_____

_____

_____

_____

_____

_____

_____

_____

_____

_____

_____

_____

**Turn to "My Word List" on page 131. Write some words from the story or other words that you would like to know more about. Use a dictionary to find the meanings.**

★ To review the words in Lessons 5–8, turn to page 126. ★

# WILD RACES

**The race is on. Who will be first to cross the finish line and claim the winner's prize? It takes skill and training to be a champion.**

In Lessons 9 - 12, you will read about some unusual races. Imagine racing across the desert sand or snow-covered ground, or through the air to reach the moon. Think about races you have seen or heard about. Write your ideas on the lines below.

| **Kinds of Races** | **Where Races Are Held** |
| --- | --- |
| _____ | _____ |
| _____ | _____ |
| _____ | _____ |
| _____ | _____ |
| _____ | _____ |

★ Read the story below. Think about the meanings of the **boldfaced** words. ★

# The King's Camel Race

Picture 2,500 **camels** racing across the desert. Young Arab boys ride the humped animals, **coaxing** and urging them on. Dust clouds rise in the air. When one camel, then another, breaks out of the pack and **lunges** ahead, people cheer.

This **competition** is called the King's Camel Race. This twelve-mile event takes place every spring outside Riyadh, the capital of Saudi Arabia.

In this part of the world, camels are still very important. They are used for milk and meat and for travel in the desert. And sometimes they are raced like horses.

Because of the big prizes, many people want to win. So there are many **entries** in the race. Hundreds of other people come just to watch the **spectacle**. When the race is over, no one forgets the amazing sight.

Getting ready for the race takes work. The boys feed their camels a special mix of grains. They exercise them every day to prepare for the long race. But riding a camel is not easy. Even after weeks of practice, some boys still fall off their camels. Or they get tired of sitting on the beast and are forced to stop and **dismount**.

The top 200 riders all **qualify** for prizes from the king. But the best prizes go to the rider with the swiftest camel that **outruns** all the others. For this **champion**, the winner of the race, there is a gold dagger, money, and a truck.

★ Go back to the story. Underline the words or sentences that give you a clue to the meaning of each **boldfaced** word. ★

# CONTEXT CLUES

Read each sentence. Look for clues to help you complete each
sentence with a word from the box. Write the word on the line.

| | | | |
|---|---|---|---|
| competition | spectacle | camels | qualify |
| coaxing | entries | dismount | champion |
| outruns | lunges | | |

1. Humped animals called _____ are raced in
   the desert.

2. The Arab boys who enter the _____ are
   serious about winning the race.

3. To _____, or to show to be fit for the race,
   a boy needs a fast camel.

4. There are a great number of _____, or
   people in the contest, because the one and only winner gets
   wonderful prizes.

5. The _____, or winner, of the camel race
   wins a truck!

6. The boy whose camel _____ all the others
   will win.

7. To urge his camel to run faster, a boy might talk to the

   beast, _____ it on.

8. A camel that obeys is the one that _____
   ahead by taking big steps.

9. A camel may stop and force its rider to get down, or

   to _____, during the race.

10. A camel race in the desert is an amazing

    _____!

# BASE WORDS

**Base words** are words without any endings or other word parts added to them. For each word below, write its base word next to it on the line. Remember, sometimes the spelling of the base word changes when an ending is added to it. Turn to the Dictionary, beginning on page 133, if you need help spelling the base words.

**1.** camels _____

**2.** coaxing _____

**3.** dismounted _____

**4.** entries _____

**5.** lunges _____

# WORD GROUPS

Read each pair of words. Think about how they are alike. Write the word from the box that best completes each group.

| spectacle | qualify | champion |
|---|---|---|
| competition | lunge | outruns |

**1.** beats, tops, _____

**2.** contest, meet, _____

**3.** winner, leader, _____

**4.** show, display, _____

**5.** pass, fit, _____

**6.** leap, spring, _____

# WORD PUZZLE

Write a word from the box next to each clue. Then read the words formed by the letters in the squares. You will have the answer to the question below.

To what part of the world would you go to see the King's

Camel Race? The _____ _____

| | | | |
|---|---|---|---|
| camel | lunges | entries | competition |
| outruns | coaxed | champion | spectacle |
| qualify | dismount | | |

1.  the winner  __ __ __ ☐ __ __ __ __

2.  those taking part in a contest  __ __ __ __ ☐ __ __

3.  to get off  ☐ __ __ __ __ __ __ __

4.  urged on  __ __ __ __ __ ☐

5.  moves forward suddenly  ☐ __ __ __ __ __

6.  contest;
    race  __ __ __ __ ☐ __ __ __ __ __

7.  a desert animal  __ __ __ ☐ __

8.  show to have the
    needed ability  __ __ ☐ __ __ __ __

9.  goes faster than others  __ __ __ __ __ __ __ ☐

10. an amazing show  __ __ __ __ ☐ __ __ __ __

**GET WISE TO TESTS**

**Directions:** Read each sentence. Pick the word that best completes the sentence. Mark the letter for that word.

Some tests put letters before the answer choices. Be sure to find the letter of the answer you think is correct and then fill in the circle beside it.

1. All _____ have one or two humps.
   A ○ riding      C ○ elephants
   B ○ camels      D ○ champion

2. The rider decided to stop and _____.
   A ○ drinking    C ○ dismount
   B ○ races       D ○ crossed

3. She finished her work so she will _____ for a prize.
   A ○ qualify     C ○ speeds
   B ○ entries     D ○ like

4. The camel _____ ahead and wins.
   A ○ quicks      C ○ pleasing
   B ○ danger      D ○ lunges

5. There are two _____ in the race.
   A ○ winning     C ○ catches
   B ○ entries     D ○ moon

6. The circus was a big _____.
   A ○ crowding    C ○ dismount
   B ○ spectacle   D ○ person

7. The _____ will be held in the gym.
   A ○ qualify     C ○ outruns
   B ○ city        D ○ competition

8. She is a _____ skater.
   A ○ champion    C ○ dirt
   B ○ coaxing     D ○ icing

9. My horse _____ the others and wins the race.
   A ○ laughed     C ○ outruns
   B ○ kicking     D ○ camels

10. He is _____ his dog to roll over.
    A ○ champion   C ○ refusing
    B ○ kitten     D ○ coaxing

**Review**

1. You _____ a house to protect it from the heat and cold.
   A ○ insulate    C ○ ruin
   B ○ painting    D ○ mature

2. A person who is very old has had a long _____.
   A ○ birth       C ○ lifetime
   B ○ normal      D ○ days

# Writing

The champion of the King's Camel Race wins a gold dagger, money, and a truck. Pretend that you are the winner of an auto race or a horse race. You have won a million dollars.

Use the lines below to write about what you would do with your prize money. Use some vocabulary words in your writing.

If I won one million dollars, I would _____

_____

_____

_____

_____

_____

_____

_____

_____

_____

Turn to "My Word List" on page 132. Write some words from the story or other words that you would like to know more about. Use a dictionary to find the meanings.

★ Read the story below. Think about the meanings of the **boldfaced** words. ★

# The Race

Determined to save his sick grandfather's farm, little Willy and his dog, Searchlight, try to win big prize money. They must outrun the best dogsled racers in the country. That includes the legendary Native American, Stone Fox, and his Samoyed dogs.

"Go, Searchlight! Go!" little Willy sang out. The snow was well packed. It was going to be a fast race today. The road was full of dangerous twists and turns, but little Willy did not have to slow down as the other **racers** did. With only one dog and a small sled, he was able to take the sharp turns at full speed without **risk** of sliding off the road or losing control.

About three miles out of town the road made a half circle around a frozen lake. Instead of following the turn, little Willy took a **shortcut** right across the lake. This was tricky going, but Searchlight had done it many times before.

Little Willy had asked Mayor Smiley if he was **permitted** to go across the lake, not wanting to be disqualified. "As long as you leave town heading north and come back on South Road," the mayor had said, "anything goes!"

None of the other racers **attempted** to cross the lake. Not even Stone Fox. The risk of falling through the ice was just too great.

Little Willy's lead increased.

At the end of five miles, little Willy was so far out in front that he couldn't see anybody behind him when he looked back.

He knew, however, that the return five miles, going back into town, would not be this easy. The trail along South Road was practically straight and very smooth, and Stone Fox was sure to close the **gap**.

Grandfather's farm was coming up.

When Searchlight saw the farmhouse, she started to pick up speed. "No, girl," little Willy yelled. "Not yet."

As they approached the farmhouse, little Willy thought he saw someone in Grandfather's bedroom window.

It couldn't be. But it was! It was Grandfather! Grandfather was sitting up in bed. He was looking out the window.

Little Willy was so excited he couldn't think straight. He started to stop the sled, but Grandfather indicated no, waving him on.

"Go, Searchlight!" little Willy **shrieked**. "Go, girl!"

Grandfather was better. Tears of joy rolled down little Willy's smiling face. Everything was going to be all right.

And then Stone Fox made his move. One by one he began to pass the other racers. Until only little Willy remained.

Little Willy still had a good lead. In fact, it was not until the last two miles of the race that Stone Fox got his first **glimpse** of little Willy since the race had begun.

The five Samoyeds looked magnificent as they moved effortlessly across the snow. Stone Fox was **gaining**, and he was gaining fast. And little Willy wasn't aware of it.

Finally little Willy glanced back over his shoulder. He couldn't believe what he saw! Stone Fox was nearly on top of him!

The lead Samoyed passed little Willy and pulled up even with Searchlight. Then it was a nose ahead. But that was all. Searchlight moved forward, inching *her* nose ahead. Then the Samoyed **regained** the lead. Then Searchlight...

When you enter the town of Jackson on South Road, the first buildings come into view about a half a mile away. Whether Searchlight took those buildings to be Grandfather's farmhouse again, no one can be sure, but it was at this time that she poured on the steam. Little Willy's sled seemed to lift up off the ground and fly. Stone Fox was left behind.

**From Stone Fox, by John Reynolds Gardiner**

★ Go back to the story. Underline any words or sentences that give you clues to the meanings of the **boldfaced** words. ★

# USING CONTEXT

Meanings for the vocabulary words are given below. Go back to the story and read each sentence that has a vocabulary word. If you still cannot tell the meaning, look for clues in the sentences that come before and after the one with the vocabulary word. Write each word in front of its meaning.

| attempted | permitted | gaining | gap |
|---|---|---|---|
| racers | shortcut | regained | risk |
| glimpse | shrieked | | |

1. _____: a quicker way of doing something or of getting somewhere

2. _____: tried

3. _____: a chance of harm

4. _____: got back again

5. _____: screamed in a high voice

6. _____: a space; an opening

7. _____: coming closer; catching up with

8. _____: a quick look

9. _____: those who run in a competition

10. _____: allowed

## CHALLENGE YOURSELF

Name two things that have a <u>gap</u> between them.

_____    _____

Name two sports in which <u>racers</u> compete.

_____    _____

# ANTONYMS

**Antonyms** are words that have opposite meanings. Match the words in the box with their antonyms listed below. Write each word on the line.

| permitted | glimpse | risky | gaining |
|---|---|---|---|

**1.** stare _____

**2.** losing _____

**3.** safe _____

**4.** refused _____

# DICTIONARY SKILLS

An **entry** on a dictionary page is the base form of the word that appears in **boldface** before its meaning. Word endings that can be added to the base word come after the meaning.

Turn to the Dictionary, beginning on page 133. Write each word in the box as it appears as an entry on each dictionary page. Then write the meaning of each word.

| attempted | racers | shortcut | shrieked |
|---|---|---|---|
| regained | gap | | |

**1.** _____

**2.** _____

**3.** _____

**4.** _____

**5.** _____

**6.** _____

# GET WISE TO TESTS

**Directions:** Find the word or words that mean the same, or about the same, as the boldfaced word. Mark your answer.

 This test will show you how well you understand the meaning of the words. Think about the meaning of the **boldfaced** word before you choose your answer.

## Review

1. **coaxing** her on
   - ○ protecting
   - ○ washing
   - ○ urging
   - ○ scaring

2. to **dismount**
   - ○ get up
   - ○ get down
   - ○ sleep
   - ○ drive

3. grand **spectacle**
   - ○ show
   - ○ car
   - ○ flower
   - ○ food

4. **qualify** to join
   - ○ want
   - ○ show anger
   - ○ forget
   - ○ show to be fit

5. is the **champion**
   - ○ racer
   - ○ winner
   - ○ competition
   - ○ loser

1. **gaining** on us
   - ○ claiming
   - ○ fighting
   - ○ coming closer
   - ○ going apart

2. quick **glimpse**
   - ○ look
   - ○ question
   - ○ answer
   - ○ visit

3. **permitted** to go
   - ○ refused
   - ○ pleased
   - ○ forced
   - ○ allowed

4. a great **risk**
   - ○ picture
   - ○ chance
   - ○ pain
   - ○ prize

5. **shrieked** loudly
   - ○ clapped
   - ○ scratched
   - ○ barked
   - ○ screamed

6. **attempted** the jump
   - ○ tried
   - ○ saw
   - ○ raced
   - ○ refused

7. wide **gap**
   - ○ feet
   - ○ cut
   - ○ space
   - ○ nose

8. **racers** are off
   - ○ those who sing
   - ○ those who watch
   - ○ those who run
   - ○ those who wait

9. **regained** the lead
   - ○ remembered
   - ○ got back
   - ○ got lost
   - ○ reported

10. took a **shortcut**
    - ○ funny way
    - ○ longer way
    - ○ cleaner way
    - ○ quicker way

Newspapers often send reporters to write about a race. Imagine that you are a reporter writing about the dogsled race.

Finish the article below. Look at the pictures to help you describe what happened. Remember to tell <u>who</u>, <u>what</u>, <u>where</u>, <u>when</u>, <u>why</u>, and <u>how</u> in your story. Use some vocabulary words in your writing.

### Close Contest

Willy and his dog, Searchlight, raced against Stone Fox and

his team of Samoyeds today. _____

_____

_____

_____

_____

_____

_____

_____

_____

_____

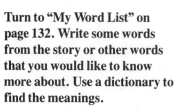

_____

_____

Turn to "My Word List" on page 132. Write some words from the story or other words that you would like to know more about. Use a dictionary to find the meanings.

_____

_____

★ Read the story below. Think about the meanings of the **boldfaced** words. ★

# The Great Space Race

Some people believe the world's greatest race is the Space Race. The United States and the Soviet Union are racing to see which country will be the first to **conquer** outer space. When did it start? On October 4, 1957, the Soviet Union sent a **satellite** named Sputnik I into space. This tiny, man-made moon sent radio signals to people in **nations** around the world. The Space Age and the Space Race had begun!

The United States had hoped to **launch** a satellite first. But there was trouble at the American rocket base when a rocket blew up. This caused a long **delay**. The United States did not send up its satellite until January 31, 1958. So the Soviet Union took the lead in the Space Race.

People around the globe wondered which country would be first to send up a **spacecraft** with a person inside. On April 12, 1961, Yuri Gagarin, a Soviet **astronaut**, circled the earth. For the second time, the Soviet Union was **triumphant**. But the United States was still close behind. One month later, Alan Shepard became the first American in space.

Now, the world wondered, which country would be the first to land a rocket on the moon. Again, the Soviets were first. But American scientists pushed hard to catch up. Finally, they jumped ahead. In December 1968, American astronauts **orbited** around the moon. Then in July of 1969, two Americans, Neil Armstrong and Edwin Aldrin, walked on the moon.

In the 1970s, both countries built space stations for gathering information. From these stations, astronauts collected **data** about outer space. As time goes by, the Space Race helps to unlock the mysteries of the stars more and more.

★ Go back to the story. Underline the words or sentences that give you a clue to the meaning of each **boldfaced** word. ★

# CONTEXT CLUES

Read each sentence. Look for clues to help you complete each sentence with a word from the box. Write the word on the line.

| | | | |
|---|---|---|---|
| spacecraft | conquer | orbited | astronaut |
| satellite | delay | nations | launch |
| triumphant | data | | |

1. The two _____ that have sent people into space are the United States and the Soviet Union.

2. They have done the most to _____, or to win victory over, this unknown region.

3. There has been more than one _____ holding up the path to victory.

4. The first step was to send a _____, a man-made moon, into space.

5. The Soviet Union was _____, or successful.

6. Today both countries _____ satellites into space.

7. Some send back _____, or information, about the weather.

8. Satellites have _____, or circled, Earth for many years.

9. It is an exciting event when a _____ with people inside it is sent into outer space.

10. It used to be that an _____ had to be a pilot, but today a scientist or engineer can be one, too.

# ANALOGIES

An **analogy** shows how two words go together in the same way as two other words. Write the words from the box to complete the following analogies.

| satellite | spacecraft | delay |
|-----------|------------|-------|
| nation    | astronaut  |       |

1. Diver is to ocean as _____ is to space.

2. Rush is to go as _____ is to stop.

3. Car is to automobile as _____ is to moon.

4. Subway is to underground as _____ is to space.

5. City is to Dallas as _____ is to the United States.

# WORD GROUPS

Read each pair of words. Think about how they are alike. Write the word from the box that completes each group.

| nations | triumphant | orbit | data |
|---------|------------|-------|------|
| launch  | conquer    |       |      |

1. countries, governments, _____

2. send, begin, _____

3. circle, ring, _____

4. facts, information, _____

5. winning, successful, _____

6. defeat, win, _____

**Directions:** Read each sentence carefully. Then choose the best answer to complete each sentence. Mark the space for the answer you have chosen.

 **Tip** If you are not sure which word completes the sentence, do the best you can. Try to choose the answer that makes the most sense.

1. To **launch** is to _____.
   A send off        C break down
   B clean up        D smash up

2. Something that has **orbited** the Earth has _____ it.
   A broken          C circled
   B forgotten       D liked

3. A **triumphant** army has been _____.
   A defeated        C stolen
   B successful      D forgotten

4. A **spacecraft** is a _____.
   A dog             C spaceship
   B creature        D walk

5. The **nations** of the world are the different _____.
   A rivers          C mountains
   B countries       D continents

6. An **astronaut** is a _____.
   A star            C spaceship
   B moon            D space traveler

7. A **delay** is a _____.
   A birth           C deal
   B wait            D dress

8. If you collect **data**, you gather _____.
   A stamps          C information
   B money           D food

9. A **satellite** is a _____.
   A planet          C hand-made lamp
   B sun             D man-made moon

10. When an army sets out to **conquer** a city, it wants to _____ it.
    A win            C find
    B lose           D build

*Writing*

Being an astronaut can mean having exciting adventures. It can also mean facing the unknown. Would you like to be an astronaut someday? Or would you like to be among the people who may live on a space station someday?

Write a paragraph explaining your feelings about being an astronaut or another kind of space traveler. Support your ideas by explaining why you would or would not like to go into space. Use some vocabulary words in your writing.

**Turn to "My Word List" on page 132. Write some words from the story or other words that you would like to know more about. Use a dictionary to find the meanings.**

★ Read the story below. Think about the meanings of the **boldfaced** words. ★

# Tarahumara Racers

It is race day for the Tarahumara Indians. Their aim is to run a 90-mile race. It will not be easy to meet their **goal**. They must run over a **rugged** mountain course. There are sharp rocks and uneven ground. They will run the course without stopping. Some will even run without shoes. It takes great **determination** to run this race. Each runner needs a strong spirit. There are many hardships to **overcome**. The runners must rise above these difficulties.

The Tarahumara live in the mountains and deep valleys of northern Mexico. Their races are an important part of their lives. The races have been held for hundreds of years. Usually there are two races a year. They celebrate times of harvest in different parts of the country.

Teams of male runners from two villages run against each other. The **opponents** play a ball game as they run. Each one uses the top of a foot to scoop up the ball and throw it. The first player to send the ball over the finish line claims **victory** for his team. His team wins!

How do the runners keep from getting tired on the 15-hour races? Many of them tie deer hooves to their belts. They fight their **weariness** by listening to the sound of the hooves beating together.

**Loneliness** is not a problem for the runners. There are always other people close by. They offer water to the strong and **hardy** runners. They also carry torches to help runners see at night. In these ways, other village members help the runners **endure** the many hardships of the race. The winners are proud of themselves. And so are the other members of the village.

★ Go back to the story. Underline the words or sentences that give you a clue to the meaning of each **boldfaced** word. ★

# USING CONTEXT

Meanings for the vocabulary words are given below. Go back to the story and read each sentence that has a vocabulary word. If you still cannot tell the meaning, look for clues in the sentences that come before and after the one with the vocabulary word. Write each word in front of its meaning.

| goal | overcome | determination | rugged |
| hardy | opponents | loneliness | endure |
| victory | weariness | | |

1. _____: wanting to be with others

2. _____: an aim; something wished for

3. _____: put up with

4. _____: the will to go on and not quit

5. _____: people trying to win the same contest

6. _____: tough; able to stand harsh conditions

7. _____: the feeling of being very tired

8. _____: rough and bumpy

9. _____: success

10. _____: conquer; defeat

# SYNONYMS

Remember that **synonyms** are words that have the same or almost the same meaning. Cross out the word in each line that is not a synonym.

1. rugged     smooth     harsh     rough

2. hardy     strong     healthy     weak

3. endure     continue     end     last

4. overcome     fail     defeat     beat

5. goal     start     aim     purpose

6. victory     failure     win     success

# DICTIONARY SKILLS

Write the words in alphabetical order, one word on each line. Then turn to the Dictionary, beginning on page 133. Find each word in the Dictionary. Write its meaning below.

| loneliness | determination | weariness | goal |
|---|---|---|---|
| victory | opponents | overcome | hardy |

1. _____

2. _____

3. _____

4. _____

5. _____

6. _____

7. _____

8. _____

# ANALOGIES

Remember that an **analogy** shows how two words go together in the same way as two other words. Write the words from the box to complete the following analogies.

| | | |
|---|---|---|
| opponents | loneliness | determination |
| victory | weariness | |

1. Friend is to enemy as _____ is to defeat.

2. Players is to game as _____ is to contest.

3. Answer is to reply as _____ is to courage.

4. Name is to title as _____ is to tiredness.

5. Hunger is to food as _____ is to friend.

# WRITING SENTENCES

Use each vocabulary word in the box to write an original sentence.

| | | |
|---|---|---|
| goal | rugged | opponents |
| victory | hardy | |

1. _____

2. _____

3. _____

4. _____

5. _____

**Directions:** Read each sentence carefully. Then choose the best answer to complete each sentence. Mark the space for the answer you have chosen.

 **Tip** Some tests have letters inside the answer circles. Fill in the circle next to your answer, covering the letter, too.

1. Her _____ is to get 100% on the test.
   A ○ school       C ○ hardy
   B ○ goal         D ○ better

2. The sharp rocks make this a _____ trail.
   A ○ endure       C ○ rugged
   B ○ happily      D ○ weariness

3. He will race against two _____.
   A ○ friend       C ○ trains
   B ○ hardy        D ○ opponents

4. Her _____ will not let her quit.
   A ○ shoes        C ○ determination
   B ○ mother's     D ○ overcome

5. A runner must be _____.
   A ○ grow         C ○ opponents
   B ○ strongly     D ○ hardy

6. A runner cannot give in to _____.
   A ○ weariness    C ○ late
   B ○ goal         D ○ lonely

7. Pain can be hard to _____.
   A ○ color        C ○ smile
   B ○ endure       D ○ loneliness

8. She must _____ her fear of animals to have a pet.
   A ○ victory      C ○ overcome
   B ○ rabbit       D ○ welcome

9. _____ makes her wish for company.
   A ○ Loneliness   C ○ Difficult
   B ○ Apples       D ○ Waited

10. A _____ makes a team happy!
    A ○ victory     C ○ defeat
    B ○ rugged      D ○ conquer

## Review

1. A runner who wins a race is _____.
   A ○ happily      C ○ triumphant
   B ○ delayed      D ○ better

2. A man-made moon is called a _____.
   A ○ sun          C ○ starry
   B ○ data         D ○ satellite

The Tarahumara run together as a team. They help each other to achieve their goal of victory.

On the lines below, write about a time when you were part of a team. A team could be you and a friend, a group of friends, or even your family. How did you work together? What was your goal? Use some vocabulary words in your writing.

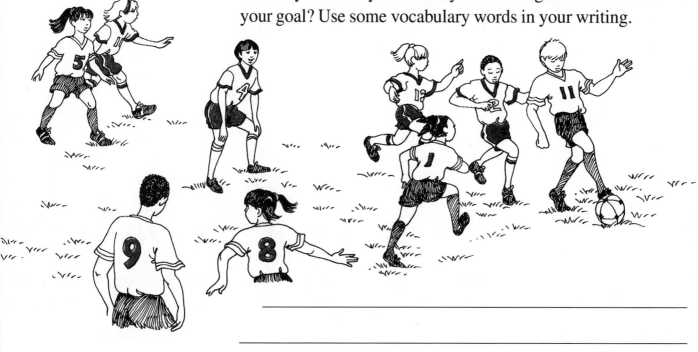

**Turn to "My Word List" on page 132. Write some words from the story or other words that you would like to know more about. Use a dictionary to find the meanings.**

★ To review the words in Lessons 9–12, turn to page 127. ★

# MOUNTAINS' MYSTERIES

**Mountains are wonders of nature. Many people enjoy the magnificent beauty of mountains. Others see a mountain and know they have to climb it.**

In Lessons 13 - 16, you will read about the wonders and mysteries of mountains. Imagine that you have climbed to the top of a very high mountain. What words describe the mountain? What words describe your feelings? Write your words under the headings below.

| The Mountain | My Feelings |
| --- | --- |
| _____ | _____ |
| _____ | _____ |
| _____ | _____ |
| _____ | _____ |

★ Read the story below. Think about the meanings of the **boldfaced** words. ★

# Climbing Mount Everest

Edmund Hillary and Tenzing Norgay push their way through the snow. They look like visitors from another planet. They wear heavy suits, hoods, and goggles. They are tied together by a 12-foot rope. The date is May 29, 1953. The two men are **ascending** Mount Everest. It is the highest mountain in the world. They hope to reach its peak today.

Mount Everest is part of the Himalaya mountain range north of India. It rises 5-1/2 miles above sea level. Near the top of the mountain, the air is thin, and breathing is hard. Temperatures drop far below freezing. The wind is fierce. Mt. Everest is a **treacherous** mountain.

Before Hillary and Norgay, seven climbing teams had tried to reach the top of Mount Everest. All of them had failed. Sixteen men had died trying to reach the **mountaintop**.

Hillary, from New Zealand, and Norgay, from Nepal, climb **uphill** slowly. They creep along at about 250 feet an hour. The last 1,100 feet are the worst. They move inch by inch up a dangerous **crest**. It crumbles under their feet. The air is so thin, they must breathe through **oxygen masks**.

The final 500-foot climb to the top is very icy. With **heroic** effort, the two men push on. As they go, they cut steps in the snow. At 11:30 A.M., they reach the top. It is a **breathtaking** view! Most people could not even imagine this sight. The two men celebrate their **arrival** by shaking hands. Below them lie the ridges and peaks of the Himalayas. Edmund Hillary and Tenzing Norgay have made history. It has been an **incredible** day.

★ Go back to the story. Underline the words or sentences that give you a clue to the meaning of each **boldfaced** word. ★

# CONTEXT CLUES

Read each sentence below. Choose a word from the box that means the same as the underlined part of each sentence. Write the word on the line after the sentence.

| | | | |
|---|---|---|---|
| incredible | arrival | crest | breathtaking |
| treacherous | heroic | oxygen masks | ascending |
| mountaintop | uphill | | |

1. It takes <u>extremely brave</u> people to try to climb Mount Everest. _____

2. Such a climb is <u>very dangerous</u>. _____

3. They are climbing <u>up the slope of a hill</u>. _____

4. Up that high, they breathe through <u>equipment that supplies the gas that all living things need</u>. _____

5. The climbers keep on <u>going up</u> anyway. _____

6. They must reach the <u>mountain's peak</u>. _____

7. The climb can offer sights that are so beautiful they are <u>hard to believe</u>. _____

8. Climbers know they are near the end of the climb when they reach <u>the top part</u> of the mountain. _____

9. Their <u>reaching of the journey's end</u> at the top means they are at the highest tip of the world. _____

10. It is a <u>thrilling and exciting</u> view from the top of Mount Everest. _____

# SYNONYMS

**Synonyms** are words that have the same or almost the same meaning. Match the words in the box with their synonyms listed below. Write each word on the line.

| mountaintop | heroic | treacherous | incredible |
|---|---|---|---|

**1.** peak _____

**2.** unbelievable _____

**3.** dangerous _____

**4.** fearless _____

# MULTIPLE MEANINGS

The words in the box have more than one meaning. Look for clues in each sentence to tell which meaning is being used. Write the letter of the meaning next to the correct sentence.

| crest | uphill | arrival |
|---|---|---|
| **a.** the top part | **a.** toward a higher place | **a.** the reaching of the journey's end |
| **b.** feathers on the head of a bird | **b.** difficult | **b.** person who arrives |

_____ **1.** A jungle bird will often have a <u>crest</u>.

_____ **2.** They were riding in on the <u>crest</u> of the wave.

_____ **3.** The plane's <u>arrival</u> has been announced.

_____ **4.** She is a new <u>arrival</u> from another country.

_____ **5.** The trail is all <u>uphill</u>.

_____ **6.** It will be an <u>uphill</u> fight to win the race.

# HIDDEN MESSAGE PUZZLE

Write a word from the box next to each clue. To find the message, copy the numbered letters in the matching numbered boxes at the bottom of the page. Then you will know where all mountain climbers want to go.

| treacherous | incredible | crest | heroic | oxygen masks |
|---|---|---|---|---|
| breathtaking | ascending | uphill | arrival | mountaintop |

1. going up ☐☐☐☐☐☐☐☐☐

2. thrilling ☐☐☐☐☐☐☐☐☐☐☐
   <sub>4</sub>

3. brave and bold ☐☐☐☐☐☐
   <sub>2</sub>

4. the top part ☐☐☐☐☐
   <sub>1</sub>

5. peak of a mountain ☐☐☐☐☐☐☐☐☐☐☐☐
   <sub>3</sub>

6. a climber's direction ☐☐☐☐☐☐
   <sub>8</sub>

7. very dangerous ☐☐☐☐☐☐☐☐☐☐☐
   <sub>6</sub>

8. used for breathing ☐☐☐☐☐☐ ☐☐☐☐☐
   <sub>7</sub>

9. the coming to a place ☐☐☐☐☐☐☐

10. impossible to believe ☐☐☐☐☐☐☐☐☐☐
    <sub>5</sub>

ANSWER: ☐☐ ☐☐☐ ☐☐☐ !
   <sub>1</sub> <sub>2</sub>   <sub>3</sub> <sub>4</sub> <sub>5</sub>   <sub>6</sub> <sub>7</sub> <sub>8</sub>

**GET WISE TO TESTS**

**Directions:** Fill in the space for the word that has the same or almost the same meaning as the boldfaced word.

Always read all the answer choices. Many choices may make sense. But only one answer choice has the same or almost the same meaning as the **boldfaced** word.

1. **treacherous** slope
   ○ safe          ○ dangerous
   ○ pretty        ○ thrilling

2. reach the **mountaintop**
   ○ peak          ○ trees
   ○ bottom        ○ movement

3. climbing **uphill**
   ○ downward      ○ faster
   ○ better        ○ higher

4. wave's **crest**
   ○ water         ○ inside
   ○ top           ○ middle

5. **incredible** view
   ○ intelligent   ○ sad
   ○ unbelievable  ○ bad

6. **ascending** the hill
   ○ going up      ○ asking
   ○ going to      ○ buying

7. **heroic** effort
   ○ weak          ○ little
   ○ heavy         ○ brave

8. **arrival** time
   ○ leaving       ○ wanting
   ○ coming        ○ waiting

9. use **oxygen masks**
   ○ breathing     ○ guns
     equipment
   ○ costumes      ○ cups

10. **breathtaking** moment
    ○ long         ○ breathing
    ○ short        ○ thrilling

**Review**

1. important **victory**
   ○ defeat        ○ vote
   ○ success       ○ person

2. **rugged** trail
   ○ rough         ○ smooth
   ○ rubber        ○ indoor

3. **overcome** fear
   ○ go by         ○ conquer
   ○ outrun        ○ have

4. **hardy** animal
   ○ weak          ○ stupid
   ○ happy         ○ strong

# *Writing*

It takes bravery to climb a mountain. It also takes bravery to do many everyday jobs, like being a fire fighter or a police officer.

On the lines below, describe a brave person you know about. The person may be a child or an adult. He or she may be someone you have met or a character on television or in a movie. Explain what the person does that makes him or her brave. Use some vocabulary words in your writing.

My idea of a brave person is _____

_____

_____

_____

_____

_____

_____

_____

_____

_____

_____

_____

_____

_____

_____

**Turn to "My Word List" on page 132. Write some words from the story or other words that you would like to know more about. Use a dictionary to find the meanings.**

★ Read the story below. Think about the meanings of the **boldfaced** words. ★

# Mountain Mist

Lost on her beloved mountain in Scotland, Meg becomes frightened as she remembers a tale her grandmother told her.

Tears welled up in Meg MacRae's eyes as she looked around her. Where were the trails and landmarks she knew so well? Only minutes before, her beloved mountain, High Crag, had been bathed in sunlight and Meg felt at home. Now the sun was **blotted** out by a low cloud. Almost immediately, the crag seemed dark and alien.

As the mist thickened and swirled around her, Meg wished very much that she had listened to her mother. Mrs. MacRae had warned her not to come up on High Crag today.

"Hear me well, lassie," her mother had said. "The Crag will be **smothered** in fog and mist afore this day is through. Should ye climb there today, ye may not see to come back down."

Meg hadn't listened, and now her mother's words had come true. Worse than that, though, was an old Scottish tale that kept repeating itself in Meg's mind. Long ago her grandmother used to tell her stories of spirits and ghosts. One especially frightened the young girl.

> *When the mist has covered all,*
> *And everything looks gray,*
> *'Tis when the Kelpies come to*
>   *call*
> *And spirit you away.*

"I'm not a wee lass anymore!" she said aloud to give herself courage. "Kelpies are only fairy tales!"

With a shake of her dark red braids, she started in what seemed to be the direction of home. Kelpies were said to be **evil** water spirits that had the shape of ponies. They would **graze** on the banks of rivers and **lochs**. When someone drowned, it was said a Kelpie had carried him away.

Finally Meg reached level ground, but the mist was still there. It was so thick she could barely see the heather on which she walked.

"I can't be far from home now." A loud splash came from the loch. Meg jumped. Then she laughed at herself. A fish must have leaped from the water to catch a tasty bug. As another sound came to her ears, Meg grew pale. Clearly through the fog, there came the sound of hoofbeats. Meg panicked. Trying to stay by the edge of the loch, she ran **desperately** away from the sound.

"Meg MacRae, Meg MacRae!" The voice sounded strange and **haunting** to Meg's frightened ears. The voice rang out again, calling her name. It began to sound familiar. She stopped altogether and tried to call out, but her voice **issued** only a quiet squeak. Clearing her throat, she tried again.

"Who is calling for Meg MacRae?" she shouted into the mist.

"Where are ye, lass?" the voice boomed. "'Tis only I, Roy Dougal. Your mother's fair worried and sent me to look."

"Roy," Meg called in relief, "I'm here, by the loch."

"Stay put, lass," Roy called. "Keep speaking, and I'll find you in a twinkling."

The hoofbeats neared, and soon Roy appeared almost magically from the mist. He was **astride** his roan **stallion**.

"Oh, Roy!" she cried. "When I heard the horse, I thought you were a Kelpie coming to get me."

"A Kelpie now, is it?" Roy exclaimed. "Don't tell me a lass such as you believes in fairy tales!"

"No, I don't. Not really," said Meg. "But everyone is afraid sometimes."

From <u>Mountain Mist</u>, by Pam Sandlin

★ Go back to the story. Underline any words or sentences that give you clues to the meanings of the **boldfaced** words. ★

# USING CONTEXT

Meanings for the vocabulary words are given below. Go back to the story and read each sentence that has a vocabulary word. If you still cannot tell the meaning, look for clues in the sentences that come before and after the one with the vocabulary word. Write each word in front of its meaning.

| | | | |
|---|---|---|---|
| smothered | graze | stallion | desperately |
| haunting | evil | blotted | astride |
| issued | lochs | | |

1. _____ : gave; sent out

2. _____ : seated with one leg on each side of something

3. _____ : to feed on grass

4. _____ : blanketed; covered thickly

5. _____ : anxiously

6. _____ : lakes in Scotland

7. _____ : a male horse

8. _____ : covered up entirely; hidden

9. _____ : wicked; very bad

10. _____ : spooky; frightening

# CHALLENGE YOURSELF

Name two animals that <u>graze</u>.

_____     _____

Name something that is <u>issued</u> daily.

_____

# ANALOGIES

An **analogy** shows how two words go together in the same way as two other words. Write the words from the box to complete the following analogies.

| loch | evil | graze | stallion | haunt |
| --- | --- | --- | --- | --- |

1. Drink is to water as _____ is to grass.

2. Prowl is to cat as _____ is to ghost.

3. Mean is to nice as _____ is to good.

4. Bull is to cow as _____ is to mare.

5. Lassie is to girl as _____ is to lake.

# DICTIONARY SKILLS

Turn to page 133 in the Dictionary. Use the **pronunciation key** to help you learn how to say the vocabulary words in ( ) in the sentences below. Write the regular spelling for each word in ( ).

1. The man (ish′ üd) a warning. _____

2. We looked (des′pər it lē) for her. _____

3. The cloud (blot′ id) out the sun. _____

4. The cake was (smu<u>th</u>′ərd) in sauce. _____

5. He sat (ə strīd′) the fence. _____

6. A thick mist covered the (lok). _____

7. The (stal′yən) is my fastest horse. _____

8. The cows (grāz) in the field. _____

9. An (ē′vəl) character scared me. _____

# GET WISE TO TESTS

**Directions:** Fill in the space for the word that fits best in the sentence.

 Be sure to mark the answer space correctly. Do <u>not</u> mark the circle with an X or with a checkmark (✔). Instead, fill in the circle neatly and completely with your pencil.

1. The warning was sent out. It was _____.
   ○ tired        ○ haunted
   ○ issued       ○ broken

2. The male horse is beautiful. It is a black _____.
   ○ stallion     ○ loch
   ○ mare         ○ calf

3. The cows will eat in this field. They will _____ here.
   ○ laugh        ○ graze
   ○ smother      ○ order

4. He tried anxiously to reach her. He was _____ concerned.
   ○ happily      ○ hardly
   ○ carefully    ○ desperately

5. We were completely covered by a pile of leaves. We were_____.
   ○ smothered    ○ grazed
   ○ standing     ○ opened

6. There are many lakes in Scotland. In that country, they are called _____.
   ○ rivers       ○ lochs
   ○ oceans       ○ stallions

7. She sat with one leg on each side of the horse. She was _____ it.
   ○ astride      ○ carrying
   ○ haunting     ○ aboard

8. The music was frightening. It sounded _____.
   ○ cheerful     ○ haunting
   ○ smothering   ○ calming

9. The witch in the story was wicked. She did _____ things.
   ○ kind         ○ funny
   ○ evil         ○ wonderful

10. You could not see the sun. The clouds _____ it out.
   ○ painted      ○ chased
   ○ issued       ○ blotted

## Writing

In the story, Meg does not pay attention to her mother's warning. She goes for a walk on the mountain and gets lost in the fog. She has to be rescued by a neighbor. Think about a time when you or someone you know did not pay attention to a warning.

On the lines below, tell about the warning and why it wasn't obeyed. What happened? Use some vocabulary words in your writing.

_____

_____

_____

_____

_____

_____

_____

_____

_____

_____

_____

_____

_____

**Turn to "My Word List" on page 132. Write some words from the story or other words you would like to know more about. Use a dictionary to find the meanings.**

★ Read the story below. Think about the meanings of the **boldfaced** words. ★

# A Wonder of Nature

The Rocky Mountains are one of nature's wonders. They are the largest mountain range in North America. They **extend** more than 3,000 miles through the western United States and Canada.

Visitors to the Rockies marvel at the spectacular mountains. If they look **upward**, they see snowcapped peaks. If they look downward from above, they see dark **gorges**. These deep, narrow openings between the sides of the mountains look as if they go on forever. If visitors were to explore the inside of these mountains, they would find huge **caverns**. These caves were formed millions of years ago along with the peaks and gorges.

How were the Rocky Mountains formed? What was their **origin**? **Geologists** who study the earth's makeup explain that the earth is always in a state of change. Inside the earth, below the top layer called the **crust**, there are layers of rock. At one time, deep inside those layers it was very hot. The rock became so hot that it was **heaved** above the crust and into the air. When the hot rock flowed down, it **deposited** high piles in some places and cut deep openings in others. When it cooled, the Rocky Mountains had been born.

Over millions of years, the forces in nature — wind, rain, and ice — shaped the mountains. This shaping made parts of the mountains smoother and rounder and other parts sharper with steep cliffs. Parts of mountains even **collapsed**, or fell in, creating bowl-shaped holes.

Whether on the ground or in the air, all who have seen the Rocky Mountains agree. They are a true wonder of nature.

★ Go back to the story. Underline the words or sentences that give you a clue to the meaning of each **boldfaced** word. ★

# CONTEXT CLUES

In each sentence, one word is underlined. That word sounds silly in the sentence. Choose a word from the box that can replace the word that sounds silly. Write it on the line.

| | | | |
|---|---|---|---|
| heaved | collapsed | gorges | geologists |
| caverns | deposited | crust | extend |
| origin | upward | | |

1. <u>Dancers</u> study mountains. _____

2. They look for the <u>peak</u>, or beginning. _____

3. They know that molten rock was thrown, or <u>skated</u>, out from inside the earth. _____

4. The rock came up through the <u>peel</u>, the top layer of the earth. _____

5. The rock that was <u>measured</u>, or left, on the earth's surface formed the Rocky Mountains. _____

6. Deep openings, or <u>doors</u>, were formed. _____

7. Caves, or <u>toys</u>, were also formed. _____

8. Bowl-shaped holes were created when sections of the mountain range fell in, or <u>crawled</u>. _____

9. The mountains seem to climb <u>slowly</u>, or toward a higher place, for miles. _____

10. The Rocky Mountains stretch out, or <u>shrink</u>, so far they cover several states! _____

# WORD GROUPS

Read each pair of words. Think about how they are alike. Write the word from the box that best completes each group.

| | | | | |
|---|---|---|---|---|
| geologist | cavern | heaved | gorge | crust |
| origin | upward | | | |

**1.** beginning, source, _____

**2.** hurled, threw, _____

**3.** teacher, astronaut, _____

**4.** uphill, uptown, _____

**5.** skin, bark, _____

**6.** cave, den, _____

**7.** canyon, valley, _____

# WRITING SENTENCES

Use each vocabulary word in the box to write an original sentence.

| | | | | |
|---|---|---|---|---|
| gorge | deposit | extend | collapse | cavern |
| origin | geologist | | | |

**1.** _____

**2.** _____

**3.** _____

**4.** _____

**5.** _____

**6.** _____

**7.** _____

**Directions:** Read each sentence carefully. Then choose the best answer to complete each sentence. Mark the space for the answer you have chosen.

**Tip** Read carefully. Use the other words in the sentence to help you choose the missing word.

1. **Gorges** are deep openings in _____.
   - (A) leaves
   - (B) oceans
   - (C) mountains
   - (D) clouds

2. A **geologist** studies the _____.
   - (A) stars
   - (B) earth
   - (C) children
   - (D) animals

3. When the house **collapsed**, it _____.
   - (A) fell in
   - (B) raised up
   - (C) came out
   - (D) went up

4. When a ball is **heaved**, it is _____ hard.
   - (A) sat on
   - (B) caught
   - (C) made
   - (D) thrown

5. When you go **upward**, you are going to a _____ place.
   - (A) lower
   - (B) higher
   - (C) darker
   - (D) shorter

6. The **crust** is the top layer of the _____.
   - (A) ocean
   - (B) clouds
   - (C) earth
   - (D) hair

7. The **origin** of something is its _____.
   - (A) beginning
   - (B) color
   - (C) death
   - (D) surface

8. Another name for **caverns** is _____.
   - (A) candles
   - (B) windows
   - (C) bats
   - (D) caves

9. Dirt **deposited** by a storm is _____ by it.
   - (A) left
   - (B) welcomed
   - (C) cut
   - (D) upside-down

10. When stores **extend** a sale, the sale is _____.
    - (A) over
    - (B) started
    - (C) stretched out
    - (D) burned out

**Review**

1. A **haunting** story is _____.
   - (A) funny
   - (B) scary
   - (C) sad
   - (D) boring

2. When horses **graze**, they _____.
   - (A) sleep
   - (B) fight
   - (C) play
   - (D) eat

Pretend that your family is planning a vacation. Some members want to go to the seashore. You want to visit the Rocky Mountains.

On the lines below, write what you would say to your family to convince everyone to go to the mountains. Give your reasons for choosing the mountains over the seashore. Use the picture to help you with details. Use some vocabulary words in your writing.

I think we should go to the mountains instead of the seashore

because _____

_____

_____

_____

_____

_____

_____

_____

_____

_____

_____

_____

**Turn to "My Word List" on page 132. Write some words from the story or other words that you would like to know more about. Use a dictionary to find the meanings.**

Pretend that your family is planning a vacation. Some members want to go to the seashore. You want to visit the Rocky Mountains.

On the lines below, write what you would say to your family to convince everyone to go to the mountains. Give your reasons for choosing the mountains over the seashore. Use the picture to help you with details. Use some vocabulary words in your writing.

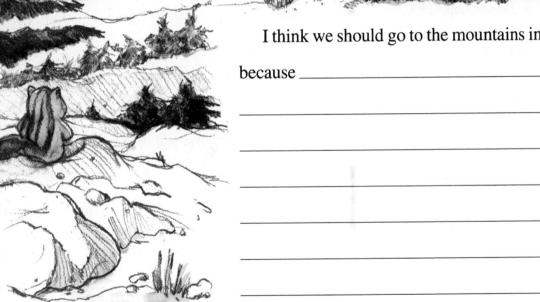

I think we should go to the mountains instead of the seashore

because _____

_____

_____

_____

_____

_____

_____

_____

_____

_____

_____

_____

**Turn to "My Word List" on page 132. Write some words from the story or other words that you would like to know more about. Use a dictionary to find the meanings.**

**Directions:** Read each sentence carefully. Then choose the best answer to complete each sentence. Mark the space for the answer you have chosen.

 **Tip** Read carefully. Use the other words in the sentence to help you choose the missing word.

1. **Gorges** are deep openings in _____.
   - (A) leaves
   - (B) oceans
   - (C) mountains
   - (D) clouds

2. A **geologist** studies the _____.
   - (A) stars
   - (B) earth
   - (C) children
   - (D) animals

3. When the house **collapsed**, it _____.
   - (A) fell in
   - (B) raised up
   - (C) came out
   - (D) went up

4. When a ball is **heaved**, it is _____ hard.
   - (A) sat on
   - (B) caught
   - (C) made
   - (D) thrown

5. When you go **upward**, you are going to a _____ place.
   - (A) lower
   - (B) higher
   - (C) darker
   - (D) shorter

6. The **crust** is the top layer of the _____.
   - (A) ocean
   - (B) clouds
   - (C) earth
   - (D) hair

7. The **origin** of something is its _____.
   - (A) beginning
   - (B) color
   - (C) death
   - (D) surface

8. Another name for **caverns** is _____.
   - (A) candles
   - (B) windows
   - (C) bats
   - (D) caves

9. Dirt **deposited** by a storm is _____ by it.
   - (A) left
   - (B) welcomed
   - (C) cut
   - (D) upside-down

10. When stores **extend** a sale, the sale is _____.
    - (A) over
    - (B) started
    - (C) stretched out
    - (D) burned out

**Review**

1. A **haunting** story is _____.
   - (A) funny
   - (B) scary
   - (C) sad
   - (D) boring

2. When horses **graze**, they _____.
   - (A) sleep
   - (B) fight
   - (C) play
   - (D) eat

★ Read the story below. Think about the meanings of the **boldfaced** words. ★

# A "Peak" Experience

A climber might be a **beginner**. She might be an expert. Either way, there is a school that will help this young person **achieve** her outdoor goals. Outward Bound offers training for many outdoor adventures, including mountain climbing. Young people might have bodies that are in really good shape, or they might not. Whether or not they have great **physical** abilities, they can learn to climb mountains.

Mountain-climbing students, in small groups, take a course that can last about three weeks. The students learn to read maps. They learn safety rules to help them **avoid** careless accidents. They pay close attention to the directions. They **concentrate** on each thing they need to learn. For example, they spend time learning the proper use of their **gear**, the equipment they need for a climb.

The students look up to their Outward Bound teachers. Each teacher is an **inspiration** to the young people. The teachers make the young people want to meet difficult challenges. They guide the students through climbing skills. They help students learn how to make choices. And they help them learn to work together.

The group works together to plan a mountain-climbing trip. When the climb is finished, the students have done something important for themselves. Everyone respects what the group has **accomplished**. Each member earns and **deserves** the praise and cheers of the teachers and other students.

Most people want to prove themselves. They have a **desire** to succeed. Outward Bound helps many young people do just that. They believe that a person who climbs a mountain can reach other peaks in life, too.

★ Go back to the story. Underline the words or sentences that give you a clue to the meaning of each **boldfaced** word. ★

# USING CONTEXT

Meanings for the vocabulary words are given below. Go back to the story and read each sentence that has a vocabulary word. If you still cannot tell the meaning, look for clues in the sentences that come before and after the one with the vocabulary word. Write each word in front of its meaning.

| concentrate accomplished beginner | gear desire physical | achieve inspiration | avoid deserves |
|---|---|---|---|

1. _____ : having to do with the body

2. _____ : someone just starting to learn something

3. _____ : to keep away from

4. _____ : equipment used for a particular purpose

5. _____ : to pay very close attention

6. _____ : a longing; a strong wish

7. _____ : a person that other people look up to

8. _____ : carried out; done

9. _____ : has a right to; is worthy of

10. _____ : to succeed in reaching a goal

# CHALLENGE YOURSELF

Name two pieces of <u>gear</u> you would take on a fishing trip.

_____     _____

Name two activities in which you are a <u>beginner</u>.

_____     _____

# MULTIPLE MEANINGS

The words in the box have more than one meaning. Look for clues in each sentence to tell which meaning is being used. Write the letter of the meaning next to the correct sentence.

| gear | concentrate | physical |
|------|-------------|----------|
| **a.** equipment | **a.** pay close attention | **a.** relating to the body |
| **b.** machine part | **b.** to bring close together in one place | **b.** a medical checkup |

_____ **1.** The airplane pilot put down the landing <u>gear</u>.

_____ **2.** Pack the camping <u>gear</u> in the trunk of the car.

_____ **3.** Sue must <u>concentrate</u> on finishing her homework.

_____ **4.** The workers will all <u>concentrate</u> in the dining room.

_____ **5.** The doctor will give her a complete <u>physical</u>.

_____ **6.** Swimming is good <u>physical</u> exercise.

# REWRITING SENTENCES

Rewrite each sentence using one of the vocabulary words from the box.

| avoid | desire | deserves |
|-------|--------|----------|

**1.** My brother is worthy of a medal for putting up with me!

_____

**2.** My dad said that we should keep away from poison ivy.

_____

**3.** To be a champion, you need the strong wish to win.

_____

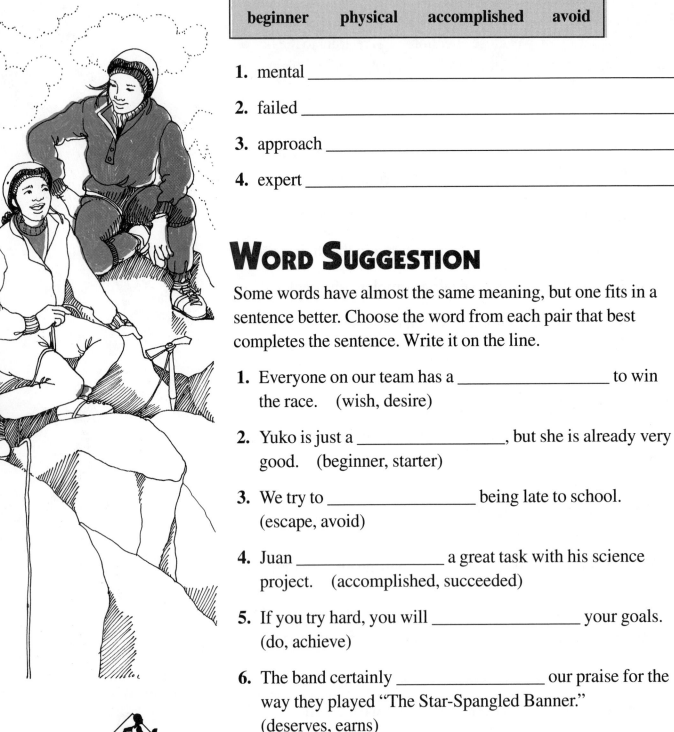

# ANTONYMS

Remember that **antonyms** are words that have opposite meanings. Match the words in the box with their antonyms listed below. Write each word on the line.

| beginner | physical | accomplished | avoid |
|----------|----------|--------------|-------|

**1.** mental _____

**2.** failed _____

**3.** approach _____

**4.** expert _____

# WORD SUGGESTION

Some words have almost the same meaning, but one fits in a sentence better. Choose the word from each pair that best completes the sentence. Write it on the line.

**1.** Everyone on our team has a _____ to win the race.   (wish, desire)

**2.** Yuko is just a _____, but she is already very good.   (beginner, starter)

**3.** We try to _____ being late to school. (escape, avoid)

**4.** Juan _____ a great task with his science project.   (accomplished, succeeded)

**5.** If you try hard, you will _____ your goals. (do, achieve)

**6.** The band certainly _____ our praise for the way they played "The Star-Spangled Banner." (deserves, earns)

**Directions:** Find the word that means the same, or about the same, as the boldfaced word. Mark your answer.

**Tip** This test will show how well you understand the meaning of the words. Think about the meaning of the **boldfaced** word before you choose your answer.

1. **concentrate** on work
   ○ rest your head
   ○ set your mind
   ○ set your clock
   ○ turn around

2. **achieve** a goal
   ○ set
   ○ reach
   ○ fail
   ○ forget

3. camping **gear**
   ○ trails
   ○ days
   ○ equipment
   ○ jokes

4. **physical** shape
   ○ mind
   ○ body
   ○ feelings
   ○ country

5. just a **beginner**
   ○ new learner
   ○ expert
   ○ manager
   ○ diver

6. **deserves** praise
   ○ needs
   ○ gives
   ○ wants
   ○ earns

7. **accomplished** much
   ○ has done
   ○ has cried
   ○ has played
   ○ has spent

8. **inspiration** to many
   ○ source of laughter
   ○ source of light
   ○ source of encouragement
   ○ source of trouble

9. **avoid** problems
   ○ rush toward
   ○ tell about
   ○ do
   ○ keep away from

10. a strong **desire**
    ○ wish
    ○ spice
    ○ rope
    ○ smell

**Review**

1. dark **caverns**
   ○ oceans
   ○ caves
   ○ roads
   ○ hills

2. mountain's **origin**
   ○ color
   ○ size
   ○ name
   ○ beginning

3. **collapsed** suddenly
   ○ fell in
   ○ sat down
   ○ drowned
   ○ raised up

4. Earth's **crust**
   ○ grass
   ○ bottom layer
   ○ pie
   ○ top layer

5. **extend** the visit
   ○ welcome
   ○ stretch out
   ○ bring out
   ○ shorten

The Outward Bound students who want to climb mountains achieve their goal. You could say that they have fulfilled a desire. What is something that you desire to do with your life?

On the lines below, tell about a goal that you would like to achieve. Why is this goal important to you? What can you do to help you fulfill your desire? Use some vocabulary words in your writing.

**Turn to "My Word List" on page 132. Write some words from the story or other words that you would like to know more about. Use a dictionary to find the meanings.**

★ To review the words in Lessons 13–16, turn to page 128. ★

# ON STAGE

**We see some shows that are live. We see others on a screen. Either way, these shows are meant to entertain us.**

In Lessons 17 - 20, you will read about different kinds of shows. Think about the shows you like. What do you like about each one? Do you like the characters or the story? Do you like the costumes or the music? Write some words that tell about the shows you like on the lines below.

**Movies and Television**               **Live Concerts**

_____     _____

_____     _____

_____     _____

_____     _____

_____     _____

★ Read the story below. Think about the meanings of the **boldfaced** words. ★

# Big Screen, Little Screen

"Ready for **broadcast**. 5 – 4 – 3 – 2 – 1! We're on the air!" The next second, television programs are brought into people's homes. This happens by sending **communication** signals through the air.

Work on televisions began in the early 1900s. But it was 1936 before people could buy them. The first show people saw on television was a cartoon.

Television started to take hold in the early 1950s. The major **networks** were in New York City. These large stations were connected to smaller stations across the country. People watched news and sports shows. Other shows were made just for people's **pleasure**. People enjoyed watching them. Many things were **advertised** for people to buy just as they are today.

Some shows were live. Others were on film. I Love Lucy was one popular show on film. It began in 1951. What made the show such a hit was Lucy. The **situations** she found herself in were like what happened to people every day. The way Lucy handled them was funny, silly, even **ridiculous**! Yet everything always worked out. Maybe that is why **generations** of people have watched the show over the years.

Beginning in the 1960s, television was not only entertaining. Viewers could also watch **educational** shows. People could learn about the world by watching television.

Big screen or little screen, it doesn't matter. Just push a button to get a different **channel**. Who knows what you will see next!

★ Go back to the story. Underline the words or sentences that give you a clue to the meaning of each **boldfaced** word. ★

# CONTEXT CLUES

Read each sentence. Look for clues to help you complete each sentence with a word from the box. Write the word on the line.

| | | | |
|---|---|---|---|
| broadcast | generations | channel | advertised |
| pleasure | communication | educational | networks |
| situations | ridiculous | | |

1. Most cities have their own television stations. These stations form large television _____ across the country.

2. Every _____ tells you something.

3. You could say that every program is a form of _____.

4. One station has the _____ programs that teach.

5. I often push the button on my television for this _____.

6. Many people enjoy watching movies or sports on television. These shows give them a lot of _____.

7. Others like funny shows where the people act silly. They laugh when the characters do _____ things on these programs.

8. Sometimes television shows remind you of events in your own life. The _____ may be very familiar.

9. Some people do not like the commercials on television. They leave the room when products are _____.

10. Television has changed since my grandmother first watched it. What will it be like for future _____?

# DICTIONARY SKILLS

Remember that **guide words** are the two words at the top of each dictionary page. They show the first and last entries on that page. All the word entries are in alphabetical order. Look at the pairs of guide words. On the lines below each pair, write the words from the box that would appear on the same dictionary page. Be sure to put them in alphabetical order.

| | | |
|---|---|---|
| channel | situation | broadcast |
| pleasure | ridiculous | generation |
| networks | communication | |

### baby / giant

1. _____

2. _____

3. _____

4. _____

### nest / strike

5. _____

6. _____

7. _____

8. _____

# BASE WORDS

Remember that **base words** are words without any endings or other word parts added to them. For each vocabulary word below, write its base word next to it on the line. Sometimes the spelling of the base word changes when an ending is added to it. Turn to the Dictionary, beginning on page 133, if you need help spelling the base words.

1. networks _____

2. communication _____

3. advertised _____

4. educational _____

# WORD MAP

Use the vocabulary words in the box to complete the word map about television. Add other words that you know to each group.

| | | | |
|---|---|---|---|
| pleasure | educational | ridiculous | broadcasts |
| situations | advertises | | |

**What You See**

1. _____

2. _____

3. _____

4. _____

**Kinds of Programs**

1. _____

2. _____

3. _____

4. _____

**TELEVISION**

**What It Gives**

1. _____

2. _____

3. _____

4. _____

**What It Does**

1. _____

2. _____

3. _____

4. _____

**Directions:** Read each sentence. Pick the word that best completes the sentence. Mark the letter for that word.

 **Tip** If you are not sure which word completes the sentence, do the best you can. Try to choose the answer that makes the most sense.

1. _____ have many stations.
   A ○ Networks    C ○ Ridiculous
   B ○ Situations    D ○ Fires

2. Some _____ are not funny.
   A ○ clowning    C ○ situations
   B ○ advertised    D ○ monkey

3. _____ has been difficult, so we have not talked.
   A ○ Count    C ○ Generations
   B ○ Speaks    D ○ Communication

4. Is this show ready for a _____?
   A ○ channels    C ○ ridiculous
   B ○ viewed    D ○ broadcast

5. My mother and I are from different _____.
   A ○ planets    C ○ moved
   B ○ generations    D ○ time

6. My pet gives me a lot of _____.
   A ○ troubling    C ○ pleasure
   B ○ bone    D ○ money

7. I saw that toy _____ on television.
   A ○ broke    C ○ make
   B ○ playful    D ○ advertised

8. I learn a lot from the _____ programs.
   A ○ educational    C ○ sported
   B ○ bake    D ○ child

9. Which _____ do you watch most?
   A ○ advertised    C ○ sound
   B ○ channel    D ○ communication

10. That silly show is _____.
   A ○ laughing    C ○ seriously
   B ○ sad    D ○ ridiculous

Think about an idea for an interesting television program for students.

   Write to the head of a television network and describe your idea. Give two reasons why the network should produce the show. Use some vocabulary words in your writing.

_____

(Date)

Dear _____ :

   I like many of the shows on your network. But I have an idea

for a new one. I think students would watch a show about \_\_\_\_\_

_____

_____

_____

_____

_____

_____

_____

_____

_____

**Turn to "My Word List" on page 132. Write some words from the story or other words you would like to know more about. Use a dictionary to find the meanings.**

_____

                    Sincerely yours,

_____

★ Read the story below. Think about the meanings of the **boldfaced** words. ★

# Popcorn

Mark Newman has big plans for his group, Popcorn. He thinks he and his friends, Missy and Richard, have the talent to make it to the top of the music world. Mark tells about a letter that just may get them on stage.

After I finished my homework that night I sat on my bed reading the music magazine that had come in the mail that day. I started to doze off, but when I actually fell asleep and rolled over, a crinkling sound woke me up. It was the junk mail Ma had said she'd left on my bed. I picked it up. The return address on the envelope was Porcupine Records Corporation. Wilshire Boulevard! Los Angeles, California! I couldn't believe that Ma would call such an incredible thing "junk mail." My heart started thumping. My eyes flew open. Suddenly I was wide awake again and my hands were trembling. I tore open the envelope and pulled out the letter. It said:

Dear Songwriter:

The **major** recording companies must continue to find and record fresh new songs. The strength of the music industry is in your hands, and that is why we are writing to you. We **urge** you to let us look over your work so that we might give you an **honest opinion**. If we decide to record your song on a commercial recording **agreement**, we will ship records to **disc jockeys** and record stores and pay you a share for each record sold. This could make you a star.

Please send us no more than three (3) of your best songs on cassette, with an **accompanying** lyric sheet for each song. As soon as we receive your material we will **review** it and you will have our opinion as quickly as possible.

Thank you. I look forward to hearing from you.

Musically yours,

William S. Shartner

Recording **Director**

From <u>Popcorn</u>, by Gary Provost
and Gail Levine-Provost

My hands were still shaking when I finished reading the letter. I read it again. How did they find out about me? I wondered. I knew this could be Popcorn's big break. I wanted to call Richard and Missy, but it was too late. I ran to the closet and lugged out my big box of cassettes. I pulled out a tape I had just made. On it were my two best songs, "Pop Some Corn," which is Popcorn's **theme** song, and "It's Good If It Goes," which is the song I wrote for my brother. I knew that both of them could be million-seller hits.

I typed up the lyric sheets for each song. That took forever because I was using my brother's old typewriter and the keys stick and besides I don't know how to type with more than one finger. Then I put everything in an envelope and addressed it to Porcupine Records. I could smell success. I wished I could run out and mail it right then. I put the package by the door so I'd be sure to mail it before school in the morning. Then I went to bed.

But I couldn't sleep. I tossed back and forth, thinking about what they had written. "The strength of the music industry is in your hands." Strength. Music industry. My hands. Strength. Music industry. My hands. Strength, music industry, my hands. And finally I fell asleep, thinking that I had found my strength.

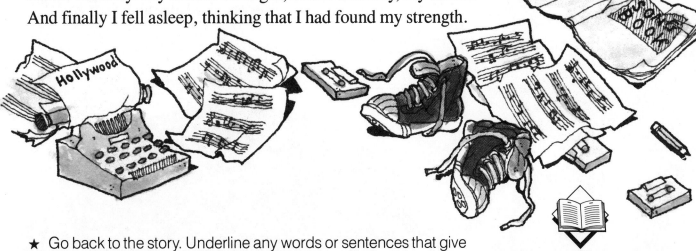

★ Go back to the story. Underline any words or sentences that give you clues to the meanings of the **boldfaced** words. ★

# USING CONTEXT

Meanings for the vocabulary words are given below. Go back to the story and read each sentence that has a vocabulary word. If you still cannot tell the meaning, look for clues in the sentences that come before and after the one with the vocabulary word. Write each word in front of its meaning.

| agreement | urge | accompanying | honest |
| director | major | disc jockeys | review |
| opinion | theme | | |

1. _____: what a person believes about something

2. _____: an understanding between two or more people

3. _____: to look at again

4. _____: full of truth

5. _____: person who manages or guides others

6. _____: melody used to identify performers or a show

7. _____: more important

8. _____: people at a radio station who play records and announce songs

9. _____: strongly encourage

10. _____: going along with

# REWRITING SENTENCES

Rewrite each sentence using one of the vocabulary words from the box.

| agreement | honest | disc jockey | accompanying |
|---|---|---|---|

1. My brother was going along with me to school.

   _____

2. Our written understanding was signed today.

   _____

3. I like the guy who announces the songs on station WXYZ.

   _____

4. He is a person who does not lie, cheat, or steal.

   _____

# SYNONYMS

**Synonyms** are words that have the same or almost the same meaning. Match the words that are synonyms.

| theme | major | review | director |
|---|---|---|---|
| urge | opinion | | |

1. manager _____

2. belief _____

3. encourage _____

4. melody _____

5. main _____

6. examine _____

# GET WISE TO TESTS

**Directions:** Fill in the space for the word that fits best in the sentence.

Before you choose an answer, try reading the sentence with each answer choice. This will help you choose an answer that makes sense.

1. She manages the business. She is the _____.
   - ○ guest
   - ○ director
   - ○ teacher
   - ○ theme

2. Mark always tells the truth. He is very _____.
   - ○ bad
   - ○ friendly
   - ○ honest
   - ○ scared

3. That company is more important. It is a _____ airline.
   - ○ major
   - ○ little
   - ○ funny
   - ○ flying

4. They will encourage her to come. I will _____ her also.
   - ○ confuse
   - ○ review
   - ○ buy
   - ○ urge

5. Amy will look over her notes again. She will _____ them for the test.
   - ○ mail
   - ○ burn
   - ○ review
   - ○ urge

6. Tim often asks me what I think. He listens to my _____.
   - ○ agreement
   - ○ dog
   - ○ stories
   - ○ opinion

7. Someone must go along with our team. Who will be _____ us?
   - ○ accompanying
   - ○ accusing
   - ○ urging
   - ○ locating

8. The composer signed the letter of understanding. Now he had an _____.
   - ○ director
   - ○ ache
   - ○ army
   - ○ agreement

9. They play records for a living. They are _____.
   - ○ majors
   - ○ disc jockeys
   - ○ directors
   - ○ composers

10. You always know her by her special melody. It is her _____.
    - ○ dress
    - ○ theme
    - ○ director
    - ○ agreement

# Writing

Along with the recording of Popcorn's theme song, Mark would have sent a letter. In the letter he would have described the group. Pretend you are Mark. What would you write to Mr. Shartner? How would you convince him to give Popcorn a chance?

Complete the letter below. Use some vocabulary words in your writing.

_____
(Date)

Mr. William S. Shartner
Porcupine Records Corporation
Wilshire Boulevard
Los Angeles, California

Dear Mr. Shartner:

The songs on this tape were recorded by Popcorn, my hot

new group. _____

_____

_____

_____

_____

_____

_____

_____

_____

**Turn to "My Word List" on page 132. Write some words from the story or other words you would like to know more about. Use a dictionary to find the meanings.**

★ Read the story below. Think about the meanings of the **boldfaced** words. ★

# Creating the Impossible

People float around rooms. Giant animals attack whole cities. Nails become claws. Faces **dissolve** before your eyes. They change into awful, watery blobs. You know these things cannot really happen. But they are happening in the movies you watch. These make-believe things are called special effects.

The **techniques**, or ways, to make what is not real seem real keep changing. The people who think of the new ideas are the **creators**. They are always trying to come up with better ideas. They want to shock, surprise, and entertain you. Many creators of special effects now use computers to make characters such as monsters and dinosaurs. The computer artist first draws a framework of the character. Then layers of details are added. The result is a dinosaur or monster that looks very real.

Some **processes** for making special effects have been around for years. For example, many effects have been done with very small models. People build the models to **represent**, or stand for, real things. Then they **assemble** them piece by piece. Later, cameras are used to film the models in different ways.

Lighting and sound have long been important in creating special effects. Lights can **flicker** quickly. Lights can **fade** into darkness. Lights can add an air of mystery. **Eerie** music with colored lights can scare you right out of your seat. The creators of special effects are very **imaginative**.

Now we all know that creepy things we see in movies are just special effects. They are not real. And we won't be scared next time we see them, will we?

★ Go back to the story. Underline the words or sentences that give you a clue to the meaning of each **boldfaced** word. ★

# USING CONTEXT

Meanings for the vocabulary words are given below. Go back to the story and read each sentence that has a vocabulary word. If you still cannot tell the meaning, look for clues in the sentences that come before and after the one with the vocabulary word. Write each word in front of its meaning.

| processes | represent | dissolve | techniques |
| imaginative | creators | eerie | fade |
| assemble | flicker | | |

1. _____ : to become less bright

2. _____ : ways of doing things; methods

3. _____ : actions done in a special order

4. _____ : able to think of new things easily

5. _____ : people who design or make things

6. _____ : to put or bring together

7. _____ : to become liquid

8. _____ : to shine with a light that is not steady; twinkle

9. _____ : causing fear; spooky

10. _____ : to stand for; to be a symbol of

## CHALLENGE YOURSELF

Name two things that you think are eerie.

_____     _____

Name two things that dissolve.

_____     _____

# SYNONYMS

Remember that **synonyms** are words that have the same or almost the same meaning. Cross out the word in each line that is not a synonym.

1. imaginative     creative     boring     clever

2. fade     darken     vanish     glitter

3. dissolve     melt     disappear     freeze

4. assemble     make     destroy     join

5. eerie     pretty     scary     strange

# DICTIONARY SKILLS

Turn to page 133 in the Dictionary. Use the **pronunciation** key to help you learn how to say the vocabulary words in ( ) in the sentences below. Write the regular spelling for each word in ( ).

1. What (pros′ es ez) did you use? _____

2. The campfire began to (flik′ ər). _____

3. The (krē ā′ tərz) are clever. _____

4. Does the flag (rep′ ri zent′) freedom? _____

5. The sun will (fād) the tent. _____

6. Watch the ice cube (di zolv′). _____

7. The door made an (îr′ e) sound. _____

8. I enjoy that artist's (tek nēk′). _____

**Directions:** Find the word that means the same, or almost the same, as the boldfaced word. Mark your answer.

**Tip** Always read all the answer choices. Many choices may make sense. But only one answer choice has the same or almost the same meaning as the **boldfaced** word.

1. monsters **dissolve**
   ○ roar
   ○ destroy
   ○ melt
   ○ sleep

2. lights **flicker**
   ○ sneeze
   ○ twinkle
   ○ break
   ○ come on

3. **imaginative** idea
   ○ dull
   ○ made up
   ○ terrible
   ○ wrong

4. **eerie** music
   ○ spooky
   ○ happy
   ○ calming
   ○ funny

5. **represent** me
   ○ deny
   ○ stand for
   ○ stand against
   ○ report

6. modern **techniques**
   ○ lights
   ○ ways
   ○ people
   ○ computers

7. talented **creators**
   ○ inventors
   ○ films
   ○ models
   ○ crayons

8. special **processes**
   ○ noises
   ○ profits
   ○ methods
   ○ actors

9. colors **fade**
   ○ become brighter
   ○ become better
   ○ become shorter
   ○ become less bright

10. **assemble** friends
    ○ attach
    ○ destroy
    ○ gather
    ○ bother

**Review**

1. **major** event
   ○ secret
   ○ magic
   ○ important
   ○ dull

2. good **director**
   ○ manager
   ○ enemy
   ○ friend
   ○ farmer

3. **urge** her
   ○ use
   ○ encourage
   ○ find
   ○ forget

4. **accompanying** us
   ○ enjoying
   ○ leaving
   ○ doing without
   ○ going along with

5. performer's **theme**
   ○ date
   ○ show
   ○ melody
   ○ jokes

Writing

Imagine you are a creator of special effects in movies. You have just been asked to make eerie special effects for a new movie. The star of the movie is your favorite actor or actress.

On the lines below, write about one of the special effects that you will use in the movie. Explain why you think your audience will like this special effect. Use some vocabulary words in your writing.

**Turn to "My Word List" on page 132. Write some words from the story or other words that you would like to know more about. Use a dictionary to find the meanings.**

_____

_____

_____

_____

_____

_____

_____

_____

_____

_____

★ Read the story below. Think about the meanings of the **boldfaced** words. ★

# Tejano Music, a New Mix

Music is coming from the stage. A band is beginning to **rehearse**, or practice, a song. Is it rock and roll? Is it country music? Is it rap? Is it jazz? The answer to all these questions is yes! The hot new sound called Tejano is a mix of all of these kinds of music. It echoes in **auditoriums** where the music is performed in many cities and towns.

Tejano music represents a mix of cultures, too. You can hear a cheerful polka beat in some of the songs. Polka music came to Texas with the German people more than 100 years ago. The words in Tejano songs can be in Spanish or in English. They can also be a mix of the two.

The word Tejano means "Texan." But it is beginning to mean more. One meaning is the special kind of music. Music lovers are loud in their praise of Tejano music. They have great interest in it. All this **enthusiasm** for the music is very strong near the border of the United States and Mexico. But the beat is becoming **internationally** known beyond these countries. A Tejano group that has recorded an **album** of songs can quickly become famous. Their tape or compact disk of songs may be played by millions of people.

Tejano music has **appeal** for young and old alike. Adults like it. Many young people in their teens are fans. These **teenagers** buy large pictures of their favorite singers. They look at these **posters** and then dress like the Tejano stars.

The crowds at Tejano events do not sit still. Chances are you will see **mobs** of people dancing when you hear the happy beat of Tejano. You will also hear long and loud clapping at the end of each song. This **applause** is for the singer, for the dancers, and for Tejano music.

★ Go back to the story. Underline the words or sentences that give you a clue to the meaning of each **boldfaced** word. ★

# CONTEXT CLUES

Read each sentence. Look for clues to help you complete each sentence with a word from the box. Write the word on the line.

| teenagers | enthusiasm | album | applause |
|---|---|---|---|
| posters | rehearse | mobs | internationally |
| appeal | auditoriums | | |

1. Many _____, often beginning at age thirteen, are starting to listen to Tejano music.

2. They show a lot of _____ for this hot new music.

3. A Tejano group that records an _____ can be known all over the world.

4. Teens like to buy _____ that have the pictures of their favorite Tejano stars on them.

5. It is not unusual to read about _____ of fans going to a Tejano concert.

6. Most concerts are held in _____, large rooms with many seats and a stage.

7. Tejano musicians must _____ often so they can put on a good show.

8. Part of the _____ of Tejano music is that it is a mix of other kinds of music.

9. The Tejano sound is becoming _____ known by people of all ages.

10. At a concert, it seems that the _____, or clapping, never seems to stop!

# SYNONYMS AND ANTONYMS

Remember that **synonyms** are words that have the same or almost the same meaning. **Antonyms** are words that have opposite meanings. Each word below is paired with a **boldfaced** vocabulary word. If the two words are synonyms, put a check (√) under that heading. If the two words are antonyms, put a (√) under that heading.

|  | Synonyms | Antonyms |
|---|---|---|
| 1. **applause** — clapping | _____ | _____ |
| 2. **internationally** — locally | _____ | _____ |
| 3. **enthusiasm** — energy | _____ | _____ |
| 4. **teenagers** — adults | _____ | _____ |
| 5. **posters** — pictures | _____ | _____ |
| 6. **appeal** — disgust | _____ | _____ |

# WORD SUGGESTION

Some words have almost the same meaning, but one fits in a sentence better. Choose the word from each pair that best completes the sentence. Write it on the line.

1. Fans filled with _____ for Tejano music live all over the world.   (interest, enthusiasm)

2. The musicians will want to _____ the music before the concert.   (rehearse, train)

3. There are three large _____ of my favorite singer covering the wall in my room.   (signs, posters)

4. There were _____ of people at the concert last night.   (mobs, herds)

# ANALOGIES

Remember that an **analogy** shows how two words go together in the same way as two other words. Write the words from the box to complete the following analogies.

| mobs | album | auditoriums | applause |
|------|-------|-------------|----------|

1. Whistling is to mouth as _____ is to hands.

2. Swarms is to bugs as _____ is to people .

3. Book is to chapter as _____ is to song.

4. Theaters is to movies as _____ is to concerts.

# DICTIONARY SKILLS

Remember that **guide words** are the two words at the top of each dictionary page. They show the first and last entries on that page. All the word entries in between are in alphabetical order. Look at the pairs of guide words. On the lines below each pair, write the words from the box that would appear on the same dictionary page. Be sure to put them in alphabetical order.

| posters | internationally | applause | appeal |
|---------|-----------------|----------|--------|
| teenagers | auditoriums | album | mobs |

| active / gain | hardy / useful |
|:-------------:|:--------------:|
| 1. _____ | 5. _____ |
| 2. _____ | 6. _____ |
| 3. _____ | 7. _____ |
| 4. _____ | 8. _____ |

**Directions:** Read each sentence carefully. Then choose the best answer to complete each sentence. Mark the space for the answer you have chosen.

Tip   Some tests have letters inside the answer circles. Fill in the circle next to your answer, covering the letter, too.

1. You **rehearse** before a _____.
   (A) concert      (C) shoe
   (B) dream        (D) cat

2. **Teenagers** are also _____.
   (A) plants       (C) houses
   (B) students     (D) schools

3. You may place **posters** on a _____.
   (A) jacket       (C) wall
   (B) nest         (D) dish

4. **Mobs** of Tejano fans can be _____.
   (A) melted       (C) noisy
   (B) adopted      (D) tasted

5. When an **album** is played, you can hear _____.
   (A) music        (C) lights
   (B) nothing      (D) chairs

6. One sign of **enthusiasm** is _____.
   (A) cheers       (C) tears
   (B) yawns        (D) anger

7. **Auditoriums** are used for _____.
   (A) accidents    (C) cooking
   (B) parking      (D) performances

8. The **appeal** of a concert is _____.
   (A) good food    (C) sound sleep
   (B) live music   (D) good sailing

9. If you are known **internationally**, you are known all over the _____.
   (A) school       (C) sky
   (B) country      (D) world

10. **Applause** is often _____.
    (A) sung        (C) repaired
    (B) tight       (D) loud

**Review**

1. Something that **flickers** _____.
   (A) bites        (C) twinkles
   (B) sleeps       (D) leaks

2. You can **assemble** a _____.
   (A) puzzle       (C) raindrop
   (B) paper        (D) breeze

Tejano music is one kind of music that people like to listen to. Some other kinds of music that people like are classical, rock, rap, and country and western. What kind of music do you like to listen to?

On the lines below, tell about your favorite kind of music. Tell why you like it, and what some of your favorite songs are. Use some vocabulary words in your writing.

**Turn to "My Word List" on page 132. Write some words from the story or other words that you would like to know more about. Use a dictionary to find the meanings.**

★ To review the words in Lessons 17–20, turn to page 129. ★

# REVIEW

Read each question. Think about the meaning of the underlined word. Then use <u>yes</u> or <u>no</u> to answer the question. Use the Dictionary if you need help.

1. If you want to visit the <u>Arctic Circle</u>, should you head for the North Pole? _____

2. Do most people in the United States eat breakfast at <u>twilight</u>? _____

3. Is it a good idea to stand close to <u>intense</u> heat? _____

4. Can a human being jump rope <u>indefinitely</u>? _____

5. Would you be likely to find a lot of <u>moisture</u> in a desert? _____

6. Would you find a <u>display</u> of light at a fireworks show? _____

7. If you want to make a doghouse <u>cheaply</u>, should you make it out of gold? _____

8. If you want to <u>focus</u> a beam of light, should you turn it off? _____

9. If a new haircut <u>transforms</u> your appearance, do you look different? _____

10. If your washing machine is broken, should you call a <u>physician</u> to repair it? _____

# REVIEW

Read each clue. Then write the word from the box that fits the clue. Use the Dictionary if you need help.

| gradual | healthy | gills | flee |
|---------|---------|-------|------|
| appetite | ignore | nerves | scrape |

1. If you are strong and well, you can use this word to describe yourself. _____

2. These parts of your body send messages to and from your brain. _____

3. If they lived only on land, tadpoles would not need these. _____

4. You might do this to a person who is boring. _____

5. If your stomach is growling and you feel hungry, you have this. _____

6. If you see lightning strike a tree beside you, you should do this. _____

7. If you do this to your knee, the nurse might put a bandage on it. _____

8. This is the kind of change that happens over millions of years. _____

# REVIEW

Read each clue. Then write the word from the box that fits the clue. Use the Dictionary if you need help.

| | | | |
|---|---|---|---|
| triumphant | opponents | champion | gap |
| spectacle | orbited | rugged | shrieked |

1. You might use this word to talk about a giant shooting star.

   _____

2. If you have ever screamed with excitement or fear, you did this. _____

3. If you want to walk on smooth ground, you should avoid this kind of path. _____

4. This is what the earth did to the sun in 365 days last year.

   _____

5. When you and a friend play each other in a game, you are these. _____

6. This is a name for the person who does not lose a contest.

   _____

7. This is probably how you would feel if you won an Olympic gold medal. _____

8. If you have this in your roof, you might get rained on.

   _____

# REVIEW

Read each clue. Then write the word from the box that fits the clue. Use the Dictionary if you need help.

| collapsed | crest | treacherous | caverns |
|-----------|-------|-------------|---------|
| avoid | gear | graze | evil |

1. If you are standing at the top of a mountain, this is where you are. _____

2. You should probably not try to canoe on this kind of river.

    _____

3. Parents often tell their children to do this to a stranger.

    _____

4. You might use this word to describe a mean character in a fairy tale. _____

5. Horses, cattle, and sheep will do this if they have grass to eat. _____

6. When people go in these, they sometimes find bats.

    _____

7. If your ladder did this, you ended up on the ground.

    _____

8. If you are going on a camping trip, you need to take this.

    _____

# REVIEW

Read each question. Think about the meaning of the underlined word. Then use <u>yes</u> or <u>no</u> to answer the question. Use the Dictionary if you need help.

1. Would you find an <u>opinion</u> in a vegetable garden?

   _____

2. If a company <u>advertised</u> a car, did they want people to buy it? _____

3. Would most people feel <u>pleasure</u> if they hit their finger with a hammer? _____

4. Would you expect an <u>honest</u> person to tell the truth?

   _____

5. If you wanted to create a video game, would an <u>imaginative</u> person come in handy? _____

6. To answer a test question correctly, should you give a <u>ridiculous</u> answer? _____

7. If you want to put a model airplane together, should you <u>assemble</u> it? _____

8. Would most people show <u>enthusiasm</u> for a meal of bread and water? _____

9. If a band wants to learn a new song, is it a good idea to <u>rehearse</u> it? _____

10. Would you expect to see <u>teenagers</u> riding tricycles?

   _____

# REVIEW AND WRITE

You have read about many places in this book. Stories have taken you from the cold of the Arctic Circle to the warmth of the Hawaiian Islands. Which of these places would people like to visit?

On the lines below, write an advertisement for one of the places you have read about. Describe what this place looks like. Tell people why they should choose it as a place to visit. Use some of the vocabulary words you have learned.

_____

_____

_____

_____

_____

_____

_____

_____

_____

_____

_____

_____

_____

_____

_____

# MY WORD LIST

This is your word list. Here you can write words from the stories. You can also write other words that you would like to know more about. Use a dictionary to find the meaning of each word. Then write the meaning next to the word.

**UNIT 1**
BRIGHT LIGHTS

**UNIT 2**
CYCLES OF CHANGE

# MY WORD LIST

**UNIT 3**
WILD RACES

_____

_____

_____

_____

_____

_____

**UNIT 4**
MOUNTAINS' MYSTERIES _____

_____

_____

_____

_____

_____

**UNIT 5**
ON STAGE

_____

_____

_____

_____

_____

# DICTIONARY

## ENTRY

Each word in a dictionary is called an **entry word**. Study the parts of an entry in the sample shown below. Think about how each part will help you when you read and write.

① **Entry Word** An entry word is boldfaced. A dot is used to divide the word into syllables.

② **Pronunciation** This special spelling shows you how to say the word. Look at the pronunciation key below. It tells you the symbols that stand for sounds.

③ **Part of Speech** The abbreviation tells you the part of speech. In this entry *v.* stands for verb.

④ **Words with Spelling Changes** When the spelling of a word changes after *-ed* or *-ing* is added, the spelling is shown in an entry.

⑤ **Definition** A definition is given for each entry word. The definition tells what the word means.

**a·chieve** (ə chēv′) *v.* **a·chieved, a·chiev·ing** To reach a goal

## PRONUNCIATION KEY

A **pronunciation key** is a helpful tool. It shows you the symbols, or special signs, for the sounds in English. Next to each symbol is a sample word for that sound. Use the key to help you with the pronunciation given after each entry word.

| | | | | |
|---|---|---|---|---|
| a | at, bad | | d | dear, soda, bad |
| ā | ape, pain, day, break | | f | five, defend, leaf, off, cough, elephant |
| ä | father, car, heart | | g | game, ago, fog, egg |
| âr | care, pair, bear, their, where | | h | hat, ahead |
| e | end, pet, said, heaven, friend | | hw | white, whether, which |
| ē | equal, me, feet, team, piece, key | | j | joke, enjoy, gem, page, edge |
| i | it, big, English, hymn | | k | kite, bakery, seek, tack, cat |
| ī | ice, fine, lie, my | | l | lid, sailor, feel, ball, allow |
| îr | ear, deer, here, pierce | | m | man, family, dream |
| o | odd, hot, watch | | n | not, final, pan, knife |
| ō | old, oat, toe, low | | ng | long, singer, pink |
| ô | coffee, all, taught, law, fought | | p | pail, repair, soap, happy |
| ôr | order, fork, horse, story, pour | | r | ride, parent, wear, more, marry |
| oi | oil, toy | | s | sit, aside, pets, cent, pass |
| ou | out, now | | sh | shoe, washer, fish, mission, nation |
| u | up, mud, love, double | | t | tag, pretend, fat, button, dressed |
| ū | use, mule, cue, feud, few | | th | thin, panther, both |
| ü | rule, true, food | | th | this, mother, smooth |
| ů | put, wood, should | | v | very, favor, wave |
| ûr | burn, hurry, term, bird, word, courage | | w | wet, weather, reward |
| ə | about, taken, pencil, lemon, circus | | y | yes, onion |
| b | bat, above, job | | z | zoo, lazy, jazz, rose, dogs, houses |
| ch | chin, such, match | | zh | vision, treasure, seizure |

# D<small>ICTIONARY</small>

## A

**ac•com•pa•ny•ing** (ə kum´pə nē ing) *adj.* Going along with. page 108

**ac•com•plish** (ə kom´plish) *v.* To do; carry out. page 95

**a•chieve** (ə chēv´) *v.* **a•chieved, a•chiev•ing** To reach a goal. page 95

**ac•tive** (ak´tiv) *adj.* Working; continuing to act. page 30

**a•dore** (ə dôr´) *v.* **a•dored, a•dor•ing** To love very much. page 36

**ad•ver•tise** (ad´vər tīz´) *v.* **ad•ver•tised, ad•ver•tis•ing** To sell a product by sending a message through television, radio, or newspapers. page 102

**a•gree•ment** (ə grē´mənt) *n.* An understanding between two or more people. page 108

**al•bum** (al´bəm) *n.* A collection of recorded songs; a phonograph record that has many songs. page 119

**al•gae** (al´jē) *n.* Small water plants. page 42

**ap•peal** (ə pēl´) *n.* Charm; attractiveness. page 119

**ap•pe•tite** (ap´i tīt´) *n.* The wish for food; hunger. page 37

**ap•plause** (ə plôz´) *n.* Clapping to show approval. page 119

**arch** (ärch) *n.* A curved shape. page 18

**Arc•tic** (ärk´tik, är´tik) *n.* The area around the North Pole. page 6

**ar•riv•al** (ə rī´vəl) *n.* The time of coming to a place; the end of a journey. page 78

**ar•tis•tic** (är tis´tik) *adj.* Done with good design and skill. page 23

**as•cend** (ə send´) *v.* To climb. page 78

**as•sem•ble** (ə sem´bəl) *v.* **as•sem•bled, as•sem•bling** To put together. page 114

**a•stride** (ə strīd´) *prep.* Sitting with one leg on each side of. page 85

**as•tro•naut** (as´trə nôt´) *n.* A person who travels on a spacecraft. page 66

**at•tempt** (ə tempt´) *v.* To try. page 60

**au•di•to•ri•um** (ô´di tôr´ē əm) *n.* A large room where people watch plays and concerts. page 119

**a•void** (ə void´) *v.* To keep away from. page 95

## B

**be•gin•ner** (bi gin´ər) *n.* A person who does something for the first time. page 95

**bi•ol•o•gist** (bī ol´ə jist) *n.* A person who studies animal life. page 42

**blot** (blot) *v.* **blot•ted, blot•ting.** To hide; cover up. page 84

**breath•tak•ing** (breth´tā´king) *adj.* Wonderful; splendid. page 78

**bright•ness** (brīt´nis) *n.* The amount of light. page 6

**broad•cast** (brôd´kast´) *n.* A program sent out by a television station. page 102

## C

**cam•el** (kam´əl) *n.* A large desert animal that has one or two humps on its back. page 54

**car•bon** (kär´bən) *n.* A very common element. Pencil leads and coal are mostly carbon. page 13

**cav•ern** (kav´ərn) *n.* A large cave. page 90

**cham•pi•on** (cham´pē ən) *n.* The winner of a contest; the person who comes in first. page 54

**chan•nel** (chan´əl) *n.* The special set of electrical waves used to send out programs from a television station. page 102

**cheap•ly** (chēp´lē) *adv.* In a way that costs little. page 12

**coax** (kōks) *v.* To urge; speak softly to persuade. page 54

**col•lapse** (kə laps´) *v.* **col•lapsed, col•laps•ing** To fall in. page 90

**com•mu•ni•ca•tion** (kə mū´ni kā´shən) *n.* Information that is sent and received. page 102

**com•pe•ti•tion** (kom´pi tish´ən) *n.* Contest; race. page 54

**con•cen•trate** (kon´sən trāt´) *v.* **con•cen•trat•ed, con•cen•trat•ing** To pay close attention to; work carefully. page 95

**con•quer** (kong´kər) *v.* To win; to gain control of. page 66

**cre•a•tor** (krē ā´tər) *n.* A person who makes something that has not been made before. page 114

**crest** (krest) *n.* The top part of a mountain. page 78

**crust** (krust) *n.* The top layer of the earth. page 90

**cur•rent** (kûr´ənt, kur´ənt) *n.* The movement of electricity through a wire. page 12

## D

**dai•ly** (dā´lē) *adj.* Happening every day. page 6

**dart** (därt) *v.* To move quickly and suddenly. page 42

**da•ta** (dā´tə, dat´ə) *n.* Facts; information. page 66

**de•lay** (di lā´) *n.* A wait until a later time. page 66

**de•pos•it** (di poz´it) *v.* To put something down. page 90

**de•serve** (di zûrv´) *v.* **de•served, de•serv•ing** To have a right to. page 95

**de•sire** (di zīr´) *n.* A strong wish; longing. page 95

**des•per•ate•ly** (des´pər it lē, des´prit lē) *adv.* In a fearful, reckless way. page 85

**de•ter•mi•na•tion** (di tûr´mə nā´shən) *n.* Great willpower in doing something. page 71

**de•vel•op•ment** (di vel´əp mənt) *n.* The process of growing up. page 42

**di•rec•tor** (di rek´tər, dī rek´tər) *n.* The person who controls and directs others' work. page 109

**disc jock•ey** (disk jok´ē) *n.* A radio announcer who plays music. page 108

**dis•mount** (dis mount´) *v.* To get down or off. page 54

**dis•play** (di splā´) *n.* A show. page 18

**dis•solve** (di zolv´) *v.* **dis•solved, dis•solv•ing** To turn into a liquid; melt. page 114

## E

**ed•u•ca•tion•al** (ej´ə kā´shə nəl) *adj.* Having to do with learning; giving knowledge. page 102

**ee•rie** (îr´ē) *adj.* Strange; scary. page 114

**en•dure** (en dûr´) *v.* **en•dured, en•dur•ing** To put up with. page 71

**en•thu•si•asm** (en thü´zē az´əm) *n.* Great interest and energy. page 119

**en•try** (en´trē) *n.* **en•tries** A person who takes part in a contest. page 54

**en•vi•ron•ment** (en vī´rən mənt, en vī´ərn mənt) *n.* The place where something lives; surroundings. page 42

**e•rupt** (i rupt´) *v.* To throw out melted rock. page 30

**e•vil** (ē´vəl) *adj.* Bad; wicked. page 84

**ex•tend** (ek stend´) *v.* To stretch in a direction. page 90

# F

**fade** (fād) *v.* **fad•ed, fad•ing** To become less bright. page 114

**flee** (flē) *v.* **fled, flee•ing** To run away. page 30

**flick•er** (flik´ər) *v.* To grow bright and dim in an unsteady way. page 114

**fo•cus** (fō´kəs) *v.* To aim a light beam in a particular direction. page 23

**func•tion** (fungk´shən) *n.* Job; usual work. page 47

**fur•nace** (fûr´nis) *n.* A box that holds a very hot fire. page 30

**fur•nish** (fûr´nish) *v.* To give. page 12

# G

**gain** (gān) *v.* To catch up; come closer. page 61

**gap** (gap) *n.* The space between two things. page 60

**gear** (gîr) *n.* Equipment. page 95

**gen•er•a•tion** (jen´ə rā´shən) *n.* All the people born about the same time. page 102

**ge•ol•o•gist** (jē ol´ə jist) *n.* A person who studies the structure of the earth. page 90

**gill** (gil) *n.* The part of a tadpole or fish that lets it breathe underwater. page 42

**gland** (gland) *n.* A part of the body that takes out materials from the blood for another use in the body. page 47

**glimpse** (glimps) *n.* A short, quick look; a glance. page 61

**goal** (gōl) *n.* Something wished for; aim. page 71

**gorge** (gôrj) *n.* A deep, narrow opening between two mountains; a steep valley. page 90

**grad•u•al** (graj´ü əl) *adj.* Happening slowly. page 42

**graze** (grāz) *v.* **grazed, graz•ing** To eat grass for food. page 84

**growth** (grōth) *n.* Process of becoming larger as time passes. page 42

# H

**har•dy** (här´dē) *adj.* **har•di•er, har•di•est** Tough; able to put up with hard conditions. page 71

**haunt•ing** (hôn´ting) *adj.* Strange and hard to forget. page 85

**health•y** (hel´thē) *adj.* **health•i•er, health•i•est** Well; free from sickness. page 47

**heave** (hēv) *v.* **heaved, heav•ing** To push. page 90

**he•ro•ic** (hi rō´ik) *adj.* Very great; far beyond the ordinary. page 78

**home•town** (hōm´toun´) *n.* The town in which a person was born. page 37

**hon•est** (on´ist) *adj.* Truthful; fair. page 108

**ho•ri•zon** (hə rī´zən) *n.* The place where earth and sky meet. page 6

**horse•shoe** (hôrs´shü´) *n.* A U-shaped metal plate that is nailed to horses' feet. page 13

# I

**ig•nore** (ig nôr´) *v.* **ig•nored, ig•nor•ing** To pay no attention to. page 36

**i•mag•i•na•tive** (i maj´ə nə tiv) *adj.* Able to think of new things easily. page 114

**im•press** (im pres´) *v.* To have a strong effect on the feelings; amaze. page 23

**in•cred•i•ble** (in kred´ə bəl) *adj.* Hard to believe. page 78

**in•def•i•nite•ly** (in def´ə nit lē) *adv.* Without any end or limit. page 13

**in•hab•it** (in hab´it) *v.* To live in or on. page 42

**in•spi•ra•tion** (in´spə rā´shən) *n.* A person who is looked up to and who makes others want to do difficult things. page 95

**in•su•late** (in´sə lāt´) *v.* **in•su•lat•ed**, **in•su•lat•ing** To keep from becoming too hot or too cold. page 47

**in•tense** (in tens´) *adj.* Very strong; very great. page 12

**in•ter•na•tion•al•ly** (in´tər nash´ə nəl ē) *adv.* Between or among nations. page 119

**in•ven•tor** (in ven´tər) *n.* A person who thinks up new devices or machines. page 13

**in•vis•i•ble** (in viz´ə bəl) *adj.* Not able to be seen. page 47

**is•sue** (ish´ü) *v.* **is•sued**, **is•su•ing** To send or give out. page 85

# L

**la•goon** (lə gün´) *n.* A small, quiet body of water connected to a larger body of water. page 42

**launch** (lônch) *v.* To send into space. page 66

**la•va** (lä´və, lav´ə) *n.* The melted rock that flows from a volcano. page 30

**life•time** (līf´tīm´) *n.* The time a person is alive. page 47

**lo•ca•tion** (lō kā´shən) *n.* Place where something is. page 6

**loch** (lok) *n. Scottish* A lake. page 85

**lone•li•ness** (lōn´lē nis) *n.* Being alone and wanting to be with others. page 71

**lunge** (lunj) *v.* **lunged**, **lung•ing** To move forward suddenly. page 54

# M

**ma•jor** (mā´jər) *adj.* Larger; more important. page 108

**man•go** (mang´gō) *n.* **man•goes** or **man•gos** The fruit of a tree that grows in the tropics. page 36

**mar•vel** (mär´vəl) *v.* To be filled with wonder; be amazed. page 23

**ma•ture** (mə chùr´, me tyùr´, mə tùr´) *adj.* Grown-up; full-grown. page 47

**mob** (mob) *n.* A large crowd. page 119

**mois•ture** (mois´chər) *n.* Wetness; dampness. page 18

**mol•ten** (mōl´tən) *adj.* Melted; turned into a liquid by heat. page 30

**moon•lit** (mün´lit´) *adj.* Lighted by the moon. page 6

**moun•tain•top** (mount´ən top´) *n.* The top of a mountain. page 78

**mulch** (mulch) *n.* Leaves or straw put around the bottom of a tree to protect it and help it grow. page 36

# N

**na•tion** (nā´shən) *n.* Country; people having the same government. page 66

**nerve** (nûrv) *n.* A body part that carries signals between the brain and spine to parts like the eyes and muscles. page 47

**net•work** (net´wûrk´) *n.* Television stations that work together to send out the same program. page 102

**night•fall** (nīt´fôl´) *n.* Dusk; the time when night comes. page 6

**nor•mal** (nôr´məl) *adj.* Usual; expected. page 47

# O

**ob•serve** (əb zûrv´) v. **ob•served, ob•serv•ing** To see; notice. page 18

**op•er•a•tor** (op´ə rā´tər) n. The person who controls a machine. page 23

**o•pin•ion** (ə pin´yən) n. What a person thinks or believes. page 108

**op•po•nent** (ə pō´nənt) n. A person you are competing against in a contest. page 71

**or•bit** (ôr´bit) v. To travel around in a circle. page 66

**or•i•gin** (ôr´i jin, or´i jin) n. Beginning; starting point. page 90

**out•run** (out´run´) v. **out•ran, out•run, out•run•ning** To run faster than. page 54

**o•ver•come** (ō´vər kum´) v. **o•ver•came, o•ver•com•ing** To get the better of; win over. page 71

**o•ver•flow** (ō´vər flō´) v. To fill up and run over. page 30

**ox•y•gen mask** (ok´sə jən mask) n. A device that gives air to mountain climbers, pilots, and others at high altitudes. page 78

# P

**per•mit** (pər mit´) v. **per•mit•ted, per•mit•ting** To let; allow. page 60

**phys•i•cal** (fiz´i kəl) adj. Having to do with the body. page 95

**phy•si•cian** (fə zish´ən). n. A doctor of medicine. page 23

**plat•i•num** (plat´ə nəm) n. A heavy silver-white precious metal. page 12

**pleas•ure** (plezh´ər) n. Enjoyment; the feeling of being pleased. page 102

**post•er** (pōs´tər) n. A large printed piece of paper that can be put up on a wall. page 119

**proc•ess** (pros´es, prō´ses) n. A group of actions done in a certain order. page 114

**pro•duce** (prə düs´, prə dūs´) v. To make; to give forth. page 23

# Q

**qual•i•fy** (kwol´ə fī´) v. **qual•i•fied, qual•i•fy•ing** To show that you are fit for something. page 54

# R

**rac•er** (rā´sər) n. A person who takes part in a contest of speed. page 60

**rain•drop** (rān´drop´) n. A drop of rain. page 18

**rain•storm** (rān´stôrm´) n. A storm that has much rain. page 18

**re•al•is•tic** (rē´ə lis´ tik) adj. Looking like real people or things; lifelike. page 23

**re•cov•er** (ri kuv´ər) v. To get well. page 37

**re•flect** (ri flekt´) v. To send back. page 18

**ref•uge** (ref´ūj) n. A place that is safe from danger. page 30

**re•gain** (rē gān´) v. To get back. page 61

**re•hearse** (ri hûrs´) v. **re•hearsed, re•hears•ing** To practice over and over. page 119

**rep•re•sent** (rep´ri zent´) v. To stand for; act in place of. page 114

**re•view** (ri vū´) v. To look at carefully. page 108

**ri•dic•u•lous** (ri dik´yə ləs) adj. Too silly to believe; laughable. page 102

**risk** (risk) n. The chance of danger or harm. page 60

**ro•bust** (rō bust´, rō´bust) adj. Healthy and strong. page 37

**rug•ged** (rug´id) adj. Rough; uneven. page 71

# S

**sat•el•lite** (sat´ə līt´) *n.* An object made by people that is sent into space by rocket. page 66

**scrape** (skrāp) *v.* **scraped, scrap•ing** To scratch; rub in a rough way. page 47

**short•cut** (shôrt´kut´) *n.* A way that is quicker or shorter. page 60

**shriek** (shrēk) *v.* To scream; make a loud, shrill sound. page 61

**sit•u•a•tion** (sich´ü ā´shən) *n.* Circumstance; problem that needs to be handled. page 102

**slope** (slōp) *n.* The side of a mountain. page 30

**smoth•er** (smuth´ər) *v.* To cover completely. page 84

**soul** (sōl) *n.* Life energy; where a person's feelings and thoughts begin. page 37

**space•craft** (spās´kraft´) *n.* Rocket; a machine that travels in space. page 66

**spec•ta•cle** (spek´tə kəl) *n.* Something to look at; an amazing sight. page 54

**spec•tac•u•lar** (spek tak´yə lər) *adj.* Wonderful to see. page 18

**spell•bound** (spel´bound´) *adj.* So interested that one cannot speak or move. page 23

**stal•lion** (stal´yən) *n.* A male horse. page 85

**sun•rise** (sun´rīz´) *n.* The appearance of the sun in the morning; the beginning of day. page 6

**sun•set** (sun´set´) *n.* The disappearance of the sun in the evening; the beginning of night. page 6

# T

**tech•nique** (tek nēk´) *n.* A way to do something; method. page 114

**teen•ag•er** (tēn´ā´jər) *n.* A person from 13 through 19 years old. page 119

**theme** (thēm) *n.* A melody that identifies a show or musical group. page 109

**trans•form** (trans fôrm´) *v.* To change greatly. page 23

**treach•er•ous** (trech´ər əs) *adj.* Dangerous. page 78

**tri•um•phant** (trī um´fənt) *adj.* Successful. page 66

**twi•light** (twī´līt´) *n.* The time between sunset and complete darkness. page 6

# U

**up•hill** (up´hil´) *adv.* Up the side of a mountain or hill. page 78

**up•ward** (up´wərd) *adv.* Toward a higher place. page 90

**urge** (ûrj) *v.* **urged, urg•ing** To ask or tell strongly. page 108

# V

**vic•to•ry** (vik´tə rē) *n.* **vic•to•ries** A win; success. page 71

**vis•i•ble** (viz´ə bəl) *adj.* Able to be seen. page 18

**viv•id** (viv´id) *adj.* Bright; brilliant. page 18

# W

**warn•ing** (wôr´ning) *n.* Sign of possible danger. page 30

**wea•ri•ness** (wîr´ē nis) *n.* Tiredness; worn out feeling. page 71

**wel•fare** (wel´fâr´) *n.* Health and happiness. page 37

**wiz•ard** (wiz´ərd) *n.* A person who can do magic. page 13

## UNIT 1 BRIGHT LIGHTS

### LESSON 1
**Land of the Midnight Sun**

**USING CONTEXT**
1. Arctic
2. horizon
3. sunset
4. sunrise
5. twilight
6. daily
7. nightfall
8. moonlit
9. location
10. brightness

**COMPOUND WORDS**
1. moonlit
2. nightfall
3. sunset
4. sunrise

**CLOZE PARAGRAPH**
1. Arctic
2. location
3. brightness
4. daily
5. horizon
6. twilight

**WORD PUZZLE**
1. twilight
2. nightfall
3. brightness
4. sunset
5. moonlit
6. horizon
7. Arctic
8. daily
9. locations
10. sunrise
Answer to Riddle: the son rise

**GET WISE TO TESTS**
1. daily
2. twilight
3. sunrise
4. sunset
5. Arctic
6. moonlit
7. Nightfall
8. horizon
9. brightness
10. location

**WRITING**
Answers will vary based on students' personal experiences.

### LESSON 2
**The Magic Light**

**CONTEXT CLUES**
1. inventor
2. wizard
3. furnish
4. cheaply
5. indefinitely
6. platinum
7. current
8. intense
9. carbon
10. horseshoe

**ANALOGIES**
1. horseshoe
2. platinum
3. inventor
4. intense
5. cheap

**DICTIONARY SKILLS**
1. carbon
2. current
3. furnish
4. indefinitely
5. wizard

**GET WISE TO TESTS**
1. strong
2. flow
3. supply
4. creator
5. without limits
6. U-shape
7. metal
8. burned material
9. clever person
10. at low cost

**Review**
1. sundown
2. everyday
3. position
4. dawn

**WRITING**
Answers will vary based on students' personal experiences.

### LESSON 3
**Rainbows**

**USING CONTEXT**
1. visible
2. rainstorm
3. display
4. raindrop
5. vivid
6. spectacular
7. arch
8. observe
9. reflects
10. moisture

**CHALLENGE YOURSELF**
Possible responses: bus, trees; balloon, garden

**WORD GROUPS**
1. arch
2. reflects
3. observe
4. vivid
5. moisture
6. display

**CLOZE PARAGRAPH**
1. moisture
2. raindrop
3. rainstorm
4. display
5. visible
6. spectacular

**GET WISE TO TESTS**
1. C  3. B  5. B  7. C  9. D
2. D  4. C  6. A  8. D  10. A

**WRITING**
Answers will vary based on students' personal experiences.

### LESSON 4
**Lasers! Lights! Action!**

**CONTEXT CLUES**
1. produce
2. physician
3. artistic
4. realistic
5. focus
6. transforms
7. marvel
8. spellbound
9. operators
10. impress

**REWRITING SENTENCES**
1. You should see a physician about that cut on your knee.
2. In this fairy tale, the kiss from a princess transforms a frog into a prince.
3. Our town has a factory that uses iron to produce steel.

**MULTIPLE MEANINGS**
1. a  3. b  5. a
2. b  4. a  6. b

**ANALOGIES**
1. marvel
2. produce
3. artistic
4. impress

**DICTIONARY SKILLS**
1. artistic: done with good design and skill
2. focus: to aim a light beam in a particular direction
3. impress: to have a strong effect on the feelings; amaze
4. operators: people who control machines
5. physician: a doctor of medicine
6. realistic: looking like real people or things; lifelike
7. spellbound: so interested that one cannot speak or move
8. transforms: changes greatly

**GET WISE TO TESTS**
1. physician
2. realistic
3. produce
4. operators
5. focus
6. marvel
7. artistic
8. impress
9. transforms
10. spellbound

**Review**
1. vivid
2. spectacular

**WRITING**
Answers will vary based on students' personal experiences.

## UNIT 2 CYCLES OF CHANGE

### LESSON 5
**An Island Is Born**

**USING CONTEXT**
1. lava
2. warnings
3. furnace
4. molten
5. flee
6. active
7. slopes
8. refuge
9. overflows
10. erupts

**CHALLENGE YOURSELF**
Possible responses: hurricane, snowstorm; baseball, hiking

**SYNONYMS**
1. warning
2. overflows
3. erupts
4. refuge

**DICTIONARY SKILLS**
1. active
2. flee
3. furnace
4. lava
5. molten
6. slopes

**CROSSWORD PUZZLE**
Across
2. flee
6. lava
7. active
8. slopes
9. refuge
Down
1. overflows
2. furnace
3. erupts
4. molten
5. warnings

**GET WISE TO TESTS**
1. working
2. signals
3. shelter
4. melted
5. heating space
6. melted rock
7. explodes
8. run from
9. sides
10. floods

**Review**
1. aim
2. changes
3. doctor
4. fascinated

**WRITING**
Answers will vary based on students' personal experiences.

### LESSON 6
**The Mango Tree**

**CONTEXT CLUES**
1. mango
2. mulch
3. soul
4. adores
5. welfare
6. ignore
7. appetite
8. robust
9. hometown
10. recover

**MULTIPLE MEANINGS**
1. b  3. a  5. b
2. a  4. b  6. a

## CLASSIFYING
mulch, mango; robust, welfare; ignore; hometown; adore

## GET WISE TO TESTS
1. B   3. A   5. C   7. C   9. D
2. A   4. D   6. C   8. B   10. B

## WRITING
Answers will vary based on students' personal experiences.

## LESSON 7
### From Tadpole to Frog
### CONTEXT CLUES
1. biologists   6. gills
2. lagoons      7. algae
3. inhabit      8. gradual
4. development  9. darts
5. growth       10. environment

### SCIENCE WORDS
1. inhabit        4. environment
2. algae          5. biologist
3. development

### ANALOGIES
1. gills      4. gradual
2. lagoons    5. growth
3. darts

### GET WISE TO TESTS
1. B   3. D   5. D   7. A   9. C
2. C   4. A   6. B   8. D   10. D

### Review
1. B   2. C   3. D   4. A

### WRITING
Answers will vary based on students' personal experiences.

## LESSON 8
### How Does Your Skin Grow?
### USING CONTEXT
1. lifetime   6. glands
2. scrape     7. insulate
3. normal     8. healthy
4. nerves     9. invisible
5. function   10. mature

### CHALLENGE YOURSELF
Possible responses: eat well, bathe; gloves, scarf

### SYNONYMS
1. normal     4. healthy
2. function   5. mature
3. invisible  6. scrape

### WRITING SENTENCES
Answers will vary based on students' personal experiences.

### WORD MAP
Parts of the Body: glands, nerves
How a Body Can Look: mature, normal, healthy
Additional answers will vary based on students' personal experiences.

### GET WISE TO TESTS
1. organs      6. well
2. full-grown  7. length of life
3. purpose     8. usual
4. unseen      9. scratch
5. protect     10. body parts

### Review
1. live in    3. moves quickly
2. slow       4. breathing organs

## WRITING
Answers will vary based on students' personal experiences.

# UNIT 3 WILD RACES

## LESSON 9
### The King's Camel Race
### CONTEXT CLUES
1. camels        6. outruns
2. competition   7. coaxing
3. qualify       8. lunges
4. entries       9. dismount
5. champion      10. spectacle

### BASE WORDS
1. camel   4. entry
2. coax    5. lunge
3. mount

### WORD GROUPS
1. outruns       4. spectacle
2. competition   5. qualify
3. champion      6. lunge

### WORD PUZZLE
1. champion    6. competition
2. entries     7. camel
3. dismount    8. qualify
4. coaxed      9. outruns
5. lunges      10. spectacle
Answer to Riddle: Middle East

### GET WISE TO TESTS
1. B   3. A   5. B   7. D   9. C
2. C   4. D   6. B   8. A   10. D

### Review
1. A   2. C

### WRITING
Answers will vary based on students' personal experiences.

## LESSON 10
### The Race
### USING CONTEXT
1. shortcut    6. gap
2. attempted   7. gaining
3. risk        8. glimpse
4. regained    9. racers
5. shrieked    10. permitted

### CHALLENGE YOURSELF
Possible responses: buildings, mountains; skating, swimming

### ANTONYMS
1. glimpse    3. risky
2. gaining    4. permitted

### DICTIONARY SKILLS
1. attempt: to try
2. regain: to get back again
3. racer: a person who takes part in a contest of speed
4. gap: the space between two things
5. shortcut: a way that is quicker or shorter
6. shriek: to scream; make a loud, shrill sound

### GET WISE TO TESTS
1. coming closer   6. tried
2. look            7. space
3. allowed         8. those who run
4. chance          9. got back
5. screamed        10. quicker way

## Review
1. urging     4. show to be fit
2. get down   5. winner
3. show

## WRITING
Answers will vary based on students' personal experiences.

## LESSON 11
### The Great Space Race
### CONTEXT CLUES
1. nations       6. launch
2. conquer       7. data
3. delay         8. orbited
4. satellite     9. spacecraft
5. triumphant    10. astronaut

### ANALOGIES
1. astronaut   4. spacecraft
2. delay       5. nation
3. satellite

### WORD GROUPS
1. nations   4. data
2. launch    5. triumphant
3. orbit     6. conquer

### GET WISE TO TESTS
1. A   3. B   5. B   7. B   9. D
2. C   4. C   6. D   8. C   10. A

### WRITING
Answers will vary based on students' personal experiences.

## LESSON 12
### Tarahumara Racers
### USING CONTEXT
1. loneliness      6. hardy
2. goal            7. weariness
3. endure          8. rugged
4. determination   9. victory
5. opponents       10. overcome

### SYNONYMS
1. smooth   4. fail
2. weak     5. start
3. end      6. failure

### DICTIONARY SKILLS
1. determination: great willpower in doing something
2. goal: something wished for; aim
3. hardy: tough; able to put up with hard conditions
4. loneliness: being alone and wanting to be with others
5. opponents: persons you are competing against in a contest
6. overcome: to get the better of; win over
7. victory: a win; success
8. weariness; tiredness; worn out feeling

### ANALOGIES
1. victory     4. weariness
2. opponents   5. loneliness
3. determination

### WRITING SENTENCES
Answers will vary based on students' personal experiences.

### GET WISE TO TESTS
1. B   3. D   5. D   7. B   9. A
2. C   4. C   6. A   8. C   10. A

### Review
1. C   2. D

**142**

## UNIT 4 MOUNTAINS' MYSTERIES

### LESSON 13
### Climbing Mount Everest
#### CONTEXT CLUES
1. heroic
2. treacherous
3. uphill
4. oxygen masks
5. ascending
6. mountaintop
7. incredible
8. crest
9. arrival
10. breathtaking

#### SYNONYMS
1. mountaintop
2. incredible
3. treacherous
4. heroic

#### MULTIPLE MEANINGS
1. b   3. a   5. a
2. a   4. b   6. b

#### HIDDEN MESSAGE PUZZLE
1. ascending
2. breathtaking
3. heroic
4. crest
5. mountaintop
6. uphill
7. treacherous
8. oxygen masks
9. arrival
10. incredible
Answer: to the top

#### GET WISE TO TESTS
1. dangerous
2. peak
3. higher
4. top
5. unbelievable
6. going up
7. brave
8. coming
9. breathing equipment
10. thrilling

#### Review
1. success
2. rough
3. conquer
4. strong

#### WRITING
Answers will vary based on students' personal experiences.

### LESSON 14
### Mountain Mist
#### USING CONTEXT
1. issued
2. astride
3. graze
4. smothered
5. desperately
6. lochs
7. stallion
8. blotted
9. evil
10. haunting

#### CHALLENGE YOURSELF
Possible responses: cow, horse; newspaper

#### ANALOGIES
1. graze
2. haunt
3. evil
4. stallion
5. loch

#### DICTIONARY SKILLS
1. issued
2. desperately
3. blotted
4. smothered
5. astride
6. loch
7. stallion
8. graze
9. evil

#### GET WISE TO TESTS
1. issued
2. stallion
3. graze
4. desperately
5. smothered
6. lochs
7. astride
8. haunting
9. evil
10. blotted

---

### LESSON 15
### A Wonder of Nature
#### CONTEXT CLUES
1. Geologists
2. origin
3. heaved
4. crust
5. deposited
6. gorges
7. caverns
8. collapsed
9. upward
10. extend

#### WORD GROUPS
1. origin
2. heaved
3. geologist
4. upward
5. crust
6. cavern
7. gorge

#### WRITING SENTENCES
Answers will vary based on students' personal experiences.

#### GET WISE TO TESTS
1. C  3. A  5. B  7. A  9. A
2. B  4. D  6. C  8. D  10. C

#### Review
1. B   2. D

#### WRITING
Answers will vary based on students' personal experiences.

### LESSON 16
### A "Peak" Experience
#### USING CONTEXT
1. physical
2. beginner
3. avoid
4. gear
5. concentrate
6. desire
7. inspiration
8. accomplished
9. deserves
10. achieve

#### CHALLENGE YOURSELF
Possible responses: fishing poles, net; playing chess, using a computer

#### MULTIPLE MEANINGS
1. b   3. a   5. b
2. a   4. b   6. a

#### REWRITING SENTENCES
1. My brother deserves a medal for putting up with me!
2. My dad said that we should avoid poison ivy.
3. To be a champion, you need the desire to win.

#### ANTONYMS
1. physical
2. accomplished
3. avoid
4. beginner

#### WORD SUGGESTION
1. desire
2. beginner
3. avoid
4. accomplished
5. achieve
6. deserves

#### GET WISE TO TESTS
1. set your mind
2. reach
3. equipment
4. body
5. new learner
6. earns
7. has done
8. source of encouragement
9. keep away from
10. wish

---

#### Review
1. caves
2. beginning
3. fell in
4. top layer
5. stretch out
#### WRITING
Answers will vary based on students' personal experiences.

## UNIT 5 ON STAGE

### LESSON 17
### Big Screen, Little Screen
#### CONTEXT CLUES
1. networks
2. broadcast
3. communication
4. educational
5. channel
6. pleasure
7. ridiculous
8. situations
9. advertised
10. generations

#### DICTIONARY SKILLS
1. broadcast
2. channel
3. communication
4. generation
5. networks
6. pleasure
7. ridiculous
8. situation

#### BASE WORDS
1. network
2. communicate
3. advertise
4. education

#### WORD GAME
What You See: situations, broadcasts
Kinds of Programs: educational, ridiculous
What It Gives: pleasure
What It Does: advertises
Additional answers will vary based on students' personal experiences.

#### GET WISE TO TESTS
1. A  3. D  5. B  7. D  9. B
2. C  4. D  6. C  8. A  10. D

#### WRITING
Answers will vary based on students' personal experiences.

### LESSON 18
### Popcorn
#### USING CONTEXT
1. opinion
2. agreement
3. review
4. honest
5. director
6. theme
7. major
8. disc jockeys
9. urge
10. accompanying

#### REWRITING SENTENCES
1. My brother was accompanying me to school.
2. Our agreement was signed today.
3. I like the disc jockey on station WXYZ.
4. He is an honest person. / He is a person who is honest.

#### SYNONYMS
1. director
2. opinion
3. urge
4. theme
5. major
6. review

#### GET WISE TO TESTS
1. director
2. honest
3. major
4. urge
5. review
6. opinion
7. accompanying
8. agreement
9. disc jockeys
10. theme

#### WRITING
Answers will vary based on students' personal experiences.

## LESSON 19
### Creating the Impossible
**USING CONTEXT**
1. fade
2. techniques
3. processes
4. imaginative
5. creators
6. assemble
7. dissolve
8. flicker
9. eerie
10. represent

**CHALLENGE YOURSELF**
Possible responses: creaking doors,
hooting owls; ice, butter

**SYNONYMS**
1. boring
2. glitter
3. freeze
4. destroy
5. pretty

**DICTIONARY SKILLS**
1. processes
2. flicker
3. creators
4. represent
5. fade
6. dissolve
7. eerie
8. technique

**GET WISE TO TESTS**
1. melt
2. twinkle
3. made up
4. spooky
5. stand for
6. ways
7. inventors
8. methods
9. become less bright
10. gather

**Review**
1. important
2. manager
3. encourage
4. going along with
5. melody

**WRITING**
Answers will vary based on students'
personal experiences.

## LESSON 20
### Tejano Music, a New Mix
**CONTEXT CLUES**
1. teenagers
2. enthusiasm
3. album
4. posters
5. mobs
6. auditoriums
7. rehearse
8. appeal
9. internationally
10. applause

**SYNONYMS AND ANTONYMS**
1. synonyms
2. antonyms
3. synonyms
4. antonyms
5. synonyms
6. antonyms

**WORD SUGGESTION**
1. enthusiasm
2. rehearse
3. posters
4. mobs

**ANALOGIES**
1. applause
2. mobs
3. album
4. auditoriums

**DICTIONARY SKILLS**
1. album
2. appeal
3. applause
4. auditoriums
5. internationally
6. mobs
7. posters
8. teenagers

**GET WISE TO TESTS**
1. A   3. C   5. A   7. D   9. D
2. B   4. C   6. A   8. B   10. D

**Review**
1. C   2. A

**WRITING**
Answers will vary based on students'
personal experiences.

## UNIT 1 REVIEW
1. yes
2. no
3. no
4. no
5. no
6. yes
7. no
8. no
9. yes
10. no

## UNIT 2 REVIEW
1. healthy
2. nerves
3. gills
4. ignore
5. appetite
6. flee
7. scrape
8. gradual

## UNIT 3 REVIEW
1. spectacle
2. shrieked
3. rugged
4. orbited
5. opponents
6. champion
7. triumphant
8. gap

## UNIT 4 REVIEW
1. crest
2. treacherous
3. avoid
4. evil
5. graze
6. caverns
7. collapsed
8. gear

## UNIT 5 REVIEW
1. no
2. yes
3. no
4. yes
5. yes
6. no
7. yes
8. no
9. yes
10. no

## REVIEW AND WRITE
Answers will vary based on students'
personal experiences.